SPECTRUM

Science

Grade 6

Published by Spectrum
an imprint of Carson-Dellosa Publishing LLC
Greensboro, NC

Photo Credit: Page 112. NOAA Photo Library. Mr. Floyd Risvold, USC&GS. California, Long Beach. March 11, 1933.

Spectrum
An imprint of Carson-Dellosa Publishing LLC
P.O. Box 35665
Greensboro, NC 27425 USA

ISBN 0-7696-5366-9

5 6 7 8 9 10 WCR 14 13 12 11   053118454

Table of Contents

Lesson 1.1 — Rules to Remember

precautions: safety measures taken ahead of time

ingest: to eat or consume

reaction: the result of mixing two or more chemical substances together

Scientists working in extreme conditions need to take special precautions. Antarctica is the coldest, windiest, driest place on Earth. The world's coldest temperature, -129°F, was recorded there. Researchers can't go out when the temperatures dip that low, but they do venture outside in conditions that are quite dangerous. They wear special clothing that can protect them from frostbite and hypothermia. They must also take survival training classes and bring emergency gear—like food, tents, stoves, and radios—with them when they are working in the field. They have to stay in regular contact with their research station, too, so that someone will know if they are in trouble.

Do you know which practices are and aren't safe in a lab?

A science lab is a place where discoveries can unfold. It's also a place where injuries can occur if the proper **precautions** aren't taken. Follow these guidelines, and you'll stay safe while you're conducting your investigations.

- Before you begin working, make sure that you understand all parts of the procedure or experiment.

- Do not eat, drink, or chew gum in the lab. Even if you're careful, you might accidentally **ingest** something harmful. Before you leave the lab, wash your hands thoroughly with soap and water.

- When you have completed an experiment, check with a teacher or other adult to see how you should dispose of the materials. Chemicals should never be poured down a sink. They could mix and a dangerous **reaction** could take place. Biological materials, like the remains of a dissected frog, should not be placed in the trashcan.

- Wear appropriate protective gear when you are working in a lab. A smock or apron can protect your clothes and keep you from carrying any chemicals outside the lab. Safety glasses should be worn whenever you are working with heat, glass, or chemicals. Gloves can protect your hands from chemicals and heat.

- Do not wear baggy clothing or dangling jewelry in the lab. If you have long hair, it should be tied back. You should also wear close-toed shoes.

- Your five senses are valuable tools of observation in the lab. Use them carefully, though. Never taste anything and don't smell anything unless you are instructed to do so. Observing something visually is fine, but keep a distance of about a foot when you're dealing with chemicals. Also, remember never to look down into a container that is being heated. The substance could splatter and burn you. You could also inhale steam that chemicals produce when they are heated.

- If you are using heated glassware, be sure to keep it away from cool or cold water. The water can cause the hot glass to shatter.

- Conducting experiments can be fun, but you need to make sure that you keep your focus. The lab isn't a place for playing jokes. Distracting a friend might put both of you in danger.

Read each description below. If safe science practices are being followed, write **S** on the line. If they are not, write **US**.

1. _____ Enrique used tongs to remove the glass beaker from the boiling water and set it next to a bowl of cold water beside the sink.

2. _____ A strange smell filled the air, and Olivia leaned closer and sniffed her beaker to see if it was coming from the mixture she had just made.

3. _____ Before Meghan lit the Bunsen burner, she borrowed a rubber band from a friend and put her hair back in a ponytail.

4. _____ Quinn measured quantities of several liquids to use in her experiment while Danny told her about the movie he had seen last weekend.

5. _____ Nico finished examining the contents of the spider's egg sac, so he asked Mr. Hamish how he should dispose of it.

6. _____ Darius had something in his eye, so he put down the test tube he was holding, took out his contact lens, and then replaced it.

Now, explain how each unsafe activity could be done more safely.

7. _____

8. _____

9. _____

10. _____

Write your answers on the lines below.

11. Why is it important to avoid eating or drinking in the lab?

_____

12. Why isn't it a good idea to wear baggy clothing or dangling jewelry in the lab?

_____

13. How are precautions that researchers in the Antarctic take similar to those that students follow in a lab?

_____

Taking a Good Look at the World

observation: the act of gathering facts or making notes about events

experimentation: the act of conducting experiments

scientific method: a technique used for scientific investigation

hypothesis: a simple statement that can be tested to see if it's true or not

variables: parts of an experiment that can change and cause a change in the results

Here's a quick review of the steps in the scientific method:

- Ask a question about the world.
- Form a hypothesis that answers the question.
- Design an experiment or make observations to prove or disprove the hypothesis.
- If the hypothesis is wrong, form a new hypothesis and design new tests.
- If the hypothesis is correct, test it again to be sure you get the same results.
- Share the results with other scientists so they can test the hypothesis as well.

Why are experiments such an important scientific tool?

Scientists are like detectives trying to solve the mysteries of the universe. They use their skills to investigate what, when, where, why, and how things happen. Probably the two most important tools a scientist has at his or her disposal are **observation** and **experimentation**. They're both parts of the **scientific method**, but they definitely aren't the same thing.

Science always begins with observation. Good scientists are curious, so their observations lead to questions. The scientific method begins when a question has been asked. Then, a hypothesis can be formed. A **hypothesis** is only useful—and scientific—if it can be tested.

The best way to test a hypothesis is to design an experiment. Experiments are one of science's greatest inventions because they allow the scientist to be in control. Each experiment is carefully designed to answer just one question—is the hypothesis true or false? In nature, there are often too many **variables** to know for sure why something happened. In an experiment, the scientist can limit the number of variables. An experiment allows a scientist to see why he or she got one result instead of another.

As important as experiments are to science, they aren't always practical. For example, how does an astronomer test a star that's thousands of light-years from Earth? Observation, however, is almost always possible. Observational science uses scientific facts that are already known to answer questions about what the scientist sees.

An astronomer can't travel across space, but with observation, he or she can still discover a lot about the stars. For example, experiments on Earth have shown that when elements are burned, each one emits a very specific wavelength of color. By observing the colors of stars, astronomers can tell which chemical elements the star contains—without ever leaving our planet.

Certain types of science use observation much more than experimentation. Archeology, paleontology, and astronomy rely heavily on observing the world, and then drawing conclusions based on the evidence.

Observation is always a part of experimenting. How else would you know what happened in an experiment if you didn't observe the results? But observational science is the method you use when experimenting can't be done.

Circle the letter of the best answer to each question below.

1. Observing and experimenting are both

   a. parts of the scientific method.

   b. ways of investigating the world.

   c. examples of hypotheses.

   d. Both a and b

2. A hypothesis is

   a. a scientific question that can be answered easily.

   b. a statement that can be proven true or false.

   c. a type of experiment used in the scientific process.

   d. the end result of an experiment.

Write your answers on the lines below.

Maddie is testing different kinds of soil to see which one is the best for growing plants. She fills one cup with a mixture of soil and sand, a second cup with soil and gravel, and a third cup with soil and shredded bark. Then, she plants radish seeds in all three cups.

3. Write a possible hypothesis for Maddie's experiment.

   _____

4. What is the variable in this experiment?

   _____

5. How will observation be a part of Maddie's experiment?

   _____

Read the examples of scientific activities listed below. Write **O** on the line if the scientist is using observation. Write **E** on the line if the scientist is conducting an experiment.

6. _____ A paleontologist decides that a dinosaur is a meat-eater because it has sharp teeth.

7. _____ A physicist tests three types of gases to see which one is densest.

8. _____ A chemist mixes water and sodium to prove that an explosion will occur.

9. _____ An archaeologist digs up an arrowhead and concludes that the ancient people who used it were hunters.

On the Rise

dormant: inactive

fermentation: a chemical process in which microorganisms, like yeast or bacteria, break down sugars to form carbon dioxide, water, and alcohol

control: a test group in an experiment in which a variable is not changed; used as a basis for comparison

There are hundreds of species of yeast. Baker's yeast and brewer's yeast are the two types most commonly used in the kitchen. Yeast can be found naturally in soil and on plant leaves and flowers. It can also be found on the skin and in the intestines of warm-blooded animals, including human beings.

A gram of yeast contains about 25 billion cells. Each cell is only approximately 3/100 of an inch in diameter.

The ancient Egyptians first used yeast for baking bread thousands of years ago.

How can you inflate a balloon without blowing into it?

Have you ever baked bread before or watched someone else make it? If you have, you probably know that most types of bread contain yeast. Yeast looks similar to other powdery baking ingredients, but it's actually alive. Yeast, a type of fungus, is a microscopic organism. When it is dry, it is **dormant**, but when it becomes moist and warm, it comes to life.

Yeast is a plantlike organism, but it can't make its own food the way plants do. Instead, it feeds on sugar. As yeast breaks down the sugar to make energy, a chemical reaction called **fermentation** takes place. In the process, it creates alcohol and carbon dioxide as waste. The carbon dioxide appears as little bubbles of gas. These bubbles are what cause bread dough to rise and baked bread to have its light, spongy texture.

Experiment: Rising to the Challenge

Materials: two packets of yeast, two plastic bottles, two balloons, warm water, granulated sugar, a tablespoon, a funnel

- Pour a cup of very warm (but not hot) water into each bottle. Place a funnel over the mouth of bottle 1 and add two tablespoons of sugar. Place the cap on the bottle and shake it until the sugar dissolves.

- Open the bottle and put the funnel over the mouth again. Add the yeast and replace the cap. Swirl the mixture around in the bottle until the yeast dissolves. The water will be cloudy and have turned a light brown color. Follow the same procedure to add yeast—but not sugar—to bottle 2, the **control** bottle.

- Open each bottle and slide the end of a balloon over the bottle's mouth. Make sure that the balloons create a tight seal. If the seals aren't tight enough, use some string, a rubber band, or packing tape to create a better seal.

- Put the bottles someplace warm, like on a sunny windowsill. In about 20 minutes or so, you will notice that the balloon on top of bottle 1 has inflated. It trapped the carbon dioxide that the yeast produced during fermentation. Balloon 2 will not have inflated because yeast does not ferment and produce carbon dioxide without sugars to feed on.

In each scenario below, a variable in the experiment has been changed. On the line that follows each scenario, write a hypothesis that contains your prediction for the outcome of the experiment. Remember, a hypothesis is written in the form of a statement.

1. Boiling hot water is used in place of the warm water in the bottles.

    _____

2. Ice-cold water is used in place of the warm water in the bottles.

    _____

3. Instead of adding sugar to the bottles, a sweet liquid, such as grape juice, is added to the warm water.

    _____

4. Instead of adding sugar to the water, two tablespoons of salt are added.

    _____

5. Now, give examples of two more ways in which you could change the variables in this experiment.

    _____

    _____

Write your answers on the lines below.

6. Why is it important to have a tight seal between the balloon and the neck of the bottle?

    _____

7. What is the purpose of using a funnel in this experiment?

    _____

8. How is dry yeast different from yeast that has been combined with warm water and flour to make bread?

    _____

9. What does yeast produce during fermentation?

    _____

The Case of the Wet Windows

warped: twisted or bent out of shape

humidity: the amount of moisture in the air

molecules: small, individual pieces of matter that contain two or more atoms

condense: change from a gas into a liquid

Condensation plays an important role in Earth's water cycle. Water molecules evaporate from wet areas on Earth's surface to fill the air with moisture. Warm air near Earth's surface naturally rises through the atmosphere, carrying water molecules with it. As the air rises, it becomes cooler. This drop in temperature causes the water molecules to condense around dust particles in the air, and tiny water droplets are formed. They collect to create clouds. Eventually, the amount of water condensed into a droplet becomes too heavy, and gravity pulls it back to Earth as rain.

How were Julio's posters ruined?

It was late October in Springtown. The days were warm, but at night, the temperatures dropped into the low 40s and high 30s. The jacket Julio had worn to school that morning lay on the floor. It was late afternoon, and the sunlight streaming through the hallway windows was making him hot.

Julio was hard at work taping posters onto the glass. He and his sister had spent the previous weekend painting them. In big letters, the posters asked students to "Vote for Julio!" Julio stood back to admire their work and then grabbed his jacket and headed home.

When Julio walked into school the next morning, sunlight poured into the hallway again, but this time from the windows on the opposite side. He quickly made a shocking discovery. Someone had gotten his posters wet! The paper was **warped**, and the letters had smeared. The posters were ruined.

Julio stomped angrily to his homeroom to inform Ms. Wilson. She asked Julio to calm down and take his seat. Then, she went to investigate.

"Good morning," Ms. Wilson said, as she reentered the room. "We're going to discuss atoms this morning, but first, let me get a drink of water."

Ms. Wilson left again and soon returned carrying a glass of ice water. She set it on her desk and began teaching. About half an hour later, she picked up the glass and showed it to the class. A wet ring had formed on the desk, and the sides of the glass were dripping with water.

"Let's have a short discussion about **humidity**," Ms. Wilson suggested. "Along with nitrogen and oxygen atoms, the air around you contains water **molecules**. Whenever the temperature drops, water molecules **condense** onto surfaces. The dew you find on grass in the mornings is a result of water molecules condensing when the temperatures cooled down overnight.

"This ice water made the surface of the glass very cold," Ms. Wilson continued. "Any air coming close to the glass was cooled as well. The water molecules in the cooled air condensed onto the nearest surface, which was the glass itself. Moisture from the air collected onto the cool glass surface, and soon there was enough water to begin dripping down the sides. Julio, do you understand what I'm saying?"

Julio smiled. "I get it."

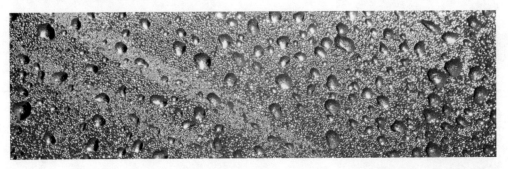

Circle the letter of the best answer to each question below.

1. Humidity refers to

    a. evaporation.

    b. the amount of moisture in the air.

    c. water that condenses onto surfaces.

    d. All of the above

2. Dew, which is the moisture found on grass in the morning,

    a. comes from inside each blade of grass.

    b. falls from the sky as small, almost invisible raindrops.

    c. is water molecules from the air that condensed.

    d. is drawn up out of the ground by changing temperatures.

3. Clouds form when

    a. wind pushes rain up into the sky.

    b. water molecules get big enough to be seen.

    c. a water molecule condenses onto a dust particle.

    d. water droplets in the atmosphere collect in large groups.

Write your answers on the lines below.

4. Explain why water condensed on the outside of Ms. Wilson's glass.

    _____

    _____

5. Explain what ruined Julio's posters.

    _____

    _____

Unifying Concepts and Processes

Do you think the temperature of Ms. Wilson's glass rose or fell as water molecules condensed onto it? Explain your answer.

_____

_____

A Sticky Lesson

fossilizing: changing into a fossil

excavating: digging up; unearthing

paleontologists: scientists who study life from past geological periods

microfossils: very small fossils, often identified with a magnifying glass or microscope

Ice Age: a period in Earth's history when temperatures dropped and part of the planet was covered in ice

Pit 91, one area of the tar pits, is still being excavated today. For two months every summer, the public can watch fossils being found. The fossils are then taken to a lab where they are cleaned using tools like dental picks, cotton swabs, and toothbrushes. Then, the fossils are identified, labeled, and cataloged.

To identify specimens, scientists compare the parts they find with fossils already in the collection. They can also compare the fossils to the skeletons of modern animals to look for similarities.

Why are the La Brea Tar Pits so important in learning about Earth's history?

Millions of years ago, before the busy city of Los Angeles existed, the area was covered by the Pacific Ocean. Over time, it turned from sea to land. Oil seeped to the surface through cracks in the ground. It pooled in the low-lying areas, which are known today as the *La Brea Tar Pits*.

During warm periods, the oil that oozed from the ground became sticky. The surface of the pools would become covered with leaves, dust, and even water. When animals came to drink, they became trapped. Predators that preyed on the trapped animals often became trapped themselves. The sticky asphalt was perfect for **fossilizing** and preserving the remains of these animals.

Today, the La Brea Tar Pits, which are actually asphalt pits, are one of the best sites for **excavating** fossils. More than three million fossils have been found there since the early 1900s. The larger fossils, which came from animals like mammoths, saber-toothed tigers, and short-faced bears, are the most dramatic findings. But fossils of plants, insects, and smaller animals are also valuable to the **paleontologists** who work in the pits.

These **microfossils** help scientists form a complete picture of what life was like in the area around Los Angeles nearly 40,000 years ago. For example, by examining plant life and even fossilized pollen, they learned that the climate was moister and cooler, but not very different than it is today. This was an important finding because an Ice Age was taking place at the time. The fossils gave scientists a better idea about the range in types of weather during an **Ice Age**.

So how do the experts know how old the fossil remains are? They use a process called *radiometric dating*. Living things contain the element *carbon*. A small portion of the carbon on Earth is an unstable isotope called *carbon-14*. Carbon-14 changes to a stable atom, but this change happens very slowly. It takes 5,730 years for half the carbon-14 to become stable. Then, it takes the same amount of time for half of the remaining carbon to become stable, and so on. Measuring the amount of unstable carbon-14 remaining in a fossil allows scientists to accurately date it. By using carbon dating on the fossils in the tar pits, they found that most were between 8,000 and 38,000 years old. This might seem ancient, but keep in mind that dinosaurs lived about 65 million years ago.

Circle the letter of the best answer to each question below.

1. Why would a scientist measure the amount of carbon-14 a fossil contains?

   a. to find out whether the fossil is authentic

   b. to find out where the fossil was found

   c. to find out what the fossil is made of

   d. to find out how old the fossil is

2. By examining the types of plant life found in the tar pits, scientists learned that during the last Ice Age, the climate in Los Angeles was

   a. very different than it is today.

   b. exactly the same as it is today.

   c. cooler and moister than it is today.

   d. hotter and drier than it is today.

Write your answers on the lines below.

3. Explain how animals became trapped in the La Brea Tar Pits.

   _____

   _____

4. Why is it helpful for scientists to study a wide variety of fossils, including microfossils?

   _____

5. What are two common tools that scientists use when cleaning fossils?

   _____

6. What sorts of comparisons do scientists make when they are trying to identify new fossils?

   _____

   _____

7. Why do you think it is important for scientists to identify, label, and catalog the specimens they find?

   _____

   _____

Pangaea, the Supercontinent

meteorologist: someone who studies meteorology, or the science of weather and Earth's atmosphere

organisms: living things, like people, plants, or animals

land bridges: pieces of land that connect two larger landmasses

continental drift: the theory that the continents drift through Earth's oceans

plate tectonics: the widely accepted theory that Earth's crust is divided into sections, called *plates,* that move around the planet; this theory has replaced the earlier, less correct theory of continental drift

In February of 2007, a stegosaurus fossil was found in Europe. Evidence of this dinosaur had never before been found outside of North America. This discovery became one more piece of evidence supporting the theory of Pangaea.

What led Alfred Wegener to the idea that Earth's continents move?

At the start of the 1900s, German **meteorologist** Alfred Wegener was fascinated by a recently discovered scientific mystery. The fossilized remains of certain plants and animals had been found on more than a single continent. For example, fossils of an extinct, freshwater reptile were discovered by archaeologists in both South America and southern Africa.

Prehistoric reptiles couldn't swim across oceans, and the exact same plant doesn't evolve in two places at once. Why were fossils of the same **organisms** appearing on continents separated by miles of ocean?

Most scientists in Wegener's day thought that the animals had crossed the oceans on **land bridges**. At certain times in Earth's history, they argued, undersea ridges became exposed when sea levels fell. The animals simply walked from one landmass to the other. Wegener wasn't so sure.

Wegener noticed that Earth's continents looked like puzzle pieces. The eastern edge of South America would fit snugly against the western edge of Africa if the continents could be put together. When Wegener did this with maps, he was amazed to see that their landscapes matched up. For example, a mountain range in South America linked perfectly to one in southern Africa. Wegener knew he was onto something.

In 1915, Wegener published his book *The Origin of Continents and Oceans*. His hypothesis stated that Earth's continents move around the planet, an idea he called **continental drift**. At one time, all the landmasses were joined together as a single supercontinent that he named *Pangaea*.

Plants and animals moved freely across Pangaea. When the supercontinent broke apart, the fossilized remains ended up on the separated continents as we know them today. Wegener argued that his idea was a much simpler solution to the fossil mystery than disappearing land bridges.

Scientists immediately ridiculed Wegener's idea. How did something as massive as an entire continent move? Wegener didn't have the answer, but he was convinced he was correct. For nearly 40 years, other scientists mostly ignored his hypothesis.

During the 1950s and 1960s, scientific equipment led to the theory of **plate tectonics**. Suddenly, Wegener's ideas weren't far-fetched at all. Today, the theory of Pangaea is widely accepted as a fact. Alfred Wegener is recognized as one of history's greatest scientists.

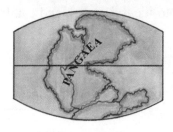  

Circle the letter of the best answer to each question below.

1. Which type of scientific research was most helpful to Wegener in forming his hypothesis?

   a. experimenting

   b. observing

   c. collecting

   d. All of the above

2. The supercontinent Pangaea

   a. is widely accepted by scientists as being part of Earth's history.

   b. is expected to reappear in about one million years.

   c. has replaced the theory of plate tectonics.

   d. was an idea that has been disproved by the theory of continental drift.

Write your answers on the lines below.

3. Explain why Wegener's ideas were suddenly accepted during the 1950s and 1960s.

   _____

   _____

4. Review the selection. Then, briefly explain why the theory of Pangaea answers the question of how the same fossils could appear on different continents.

   _____

   _____

   _____

5. Was Wegener a good scientist? Explain your answer.

   _____

   _____

What's Next?

Land bridges weren't the answer to the fossil mystery that Wegener solved, but they have existed in different places and at different times in Earth's long history. The Bering land bridge is probably the best-known link that ever arose between two continents. Why was it such an important part of early human history?

The Rise and Fall of Planet X

composition: the parts something is made of, and how the parts are put together

calculations: results or answers found by solving mathematical problems

Astronomers at the Lowell Observatory chose to name the new planet *Pluto*, which was suggested by an 11-year-old girl from England. Hundreds of different names had been sent to them for consideration, but Pluto's first two letters worked as a tribute to the man they wanted to honor—Percival Lowell.

After more than 70 years as our solar system's ninth planet, Pluto's status was recently changed to that of dwarf planet. Pluto is considered one of the largest objects in an area called the *Kuiper Belt*.

Has the mysterious Planet X been found?

By the beginning of the 1800s, astronomers had discovered seven of our solar system's planets. Each planet's mass, **composition**, and orbit were studied carefully. Astronomers noticed that Uranus's orbit was slightly different than their **calculations** predicted it should be. Their explanation was that gravity from an undiscovered planet was affecting it. New calculations were made to predict where this unknown planet might be.

On September 23, 1846, Neptune was discovered where the astronomers had said it would be. They realized that Neptune's orbit wasn't following the predicted path, either. Their explanation was yet another planet.

Astronomer Percival Lowell named this undiscovered planet *Planet X*. Lowell had used his fortune to build the Lowell Observatory in Flagstaff, Arizona. He spent nearly ten years calculating where to find the planet and observing the skies. When he died in 1916, Planet X still hadn't been found. The search stopped for more than a decade.

During the 1920s, Lowell's reputation began to suffer. One of his most famous theories had been that life existed on Mars. Lowell thought he had seen canals on the planet's surface and argued that they must have been built by intelligent creatures. By the 1920s, it was clear that no life existed on Mars, and that Lowell's "canals" were natural parts of the Martian landscape.

The new owners of the observatory wanted to restore some dignity to Lowell's name, so in 1928, they resumed searching for Planet X. A young astronomer from Kansas named Clyde Tombaugh was hired for the task.

Tombaugh used Lowell's calculations, but he also compared photos of the night sky taken one night with photos taken several nights later. He looked carefully for any points of light that had moved. Tombaugh knew that stars would be in the same position night after night, but a planet would have moved along in its orbit. On February 18, 1930, Tombaugh spotted Pluto.

Tiny Pluto wasn't nearly as massive as Lowell's Planet X was supposed to be. Was there still a giant Planet X orbiting even farther out in space? For decades this remained a mystery.

In 1989, the *Voyager 2* spacecraft flew near Neptune and sent back precise measurements of the planet's mass. Earlier calculations had been wrong. Neptune's orbit made perfect sense based on the new information and was not affected by the mysterious Planet X.

Circle the letter of the best answer to each question below.

1. Percival Lowell

   a. discovered Pluto.

   b. discovered Neptune.

   c. made predictions about where to find Planet X.

   d. Both a and c

2. Lowell's reputation suffered because

   a. he believed intelligent creatures lived on Mars.

   b. he predicted a giant Planet X existed in the solar system.

   c. Pluto wasn't found during his lifetime.

   d. Clyde Tombaugh took over his job at the observatory.

Write your answers on the lines below.

3. After Uranus was discovered, why did astronomers believe they should begin looking for another planet?

   _____

4. In order to solve the mystery of Planet X, why were observing and collecting evidence used instead of experimenting?

   _____

   _____

5. How did advances in scientific technology help solve the mystery of Planet X?

   _____

Unifying Concepts and Processes

When you think of scientific tools, you might imagine test tubes, rulers, and microscopes. A tool can be anything that helps get a job done, though. For example, math and photography were tools used to discover Pluto. Explain how they were used.

_____

_____

_____

Seeing with Electronic Eyes

optical: using light

electron: particle with a negative electrical charge found in an atom; electrons orbit the atom's nucleus, which contains protons and neutrons

pixels: small, colored dots that combine to form images on a computer or television screen

vacuum: space that is completely free of matter

freeze-dried: went through the freeze-drying process, which means all moisture was removed without damaging the original object

conductors: elements or other substances that allow electricity to easily pass through them

Electron microscopes can magnify objects up to two million times. Even the individual atoms inside certain materials can be seen with these powerful tools.

Objects also need to be good **conductors** in order to be "seen" by a beam of electrons. A freeze-dried bug wouldn't be a good conductor. Scientists coat these kinds of specimens with a thin layer of metal. Then, the electron beam has no trouble mapping the surface.

How is an optical microscope different from an electron microscope?

Optical microscopes use lenses and light to magnify objects too small to be seen with the naked eye. They help scientists peer into the miniscule worlds of bacteria, cells, and other tiny matter. The strongest optical microscopes can magnify objects up to about 1,000 times their original size. In order to see anything smaller, you need an **electron** microscope.

The amount an optical microscope can magnify something is limited because it uses light. Remember, light is a form of electromagnetic radiation, or energy that moves in waves. You see because light waves bounce off objects and then enter your eyes. When you look through a microscope, the light waves coming off a tiny object, like a cell, are magnified by the lenses and focused directly into your eye. The smallest thing that could be seen might be a large virus.

Imagine enlarging a digital photo. If you go too far, you end up with a bunch of colored dots that don't show anything. The **pixels** are too big to show the smallest details. In a similar way, light waves can only show details to a certain point.

An electron microscope solves this problem because it doesn't use light. It uses electrons. A machine shoots a very thin beam of electrons toward the object to be viewed. The beam moves slowly back and forth across the object's surface. Everywhere the beam hits, its electrons repel a few electrons off the object's surface. The microscope reads these electrons, and it uses them to make a 3-D image of the object. This image is shown on a computer monitor, or it can be used to create a photograph.

Anything that's going to be seen by an electron microscope has to be placed inside a **vacuum**. Otherwise, the beam of electrons will hit molecules in the air instead of whatever is to be magnified. Using a vacuum creates a special problem, though. Anything containing liquids or gases will quickly expand inside a vacuum.

To solve this problem, organisms are **freeze-dried** or dipped in liquid nitrogen before they are viewed. Everything viewed with an electron microscope is dead. Optical microscopes have the advantage of being used to see living cells or organisms.

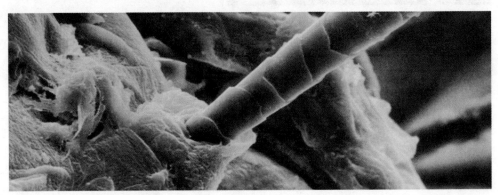

Circle the letter of the best answer to each question below.

1. Optical microscopes use _____ to magnify objects.

   a. lenses

   b. light

   c. electromagnetic radiation

   d. All of the above

2. An electron microscope shoots a _____ of electrons at the object it's magnifying.

   a. radiation

   b. beam

   c. lens

   d. pixel

Write your answers on the lines below.

3. Living organisms contain water. Why does moisture need to be removed before an organism can be viewed with an electron microscope?

   _____

   _____

4. How are optical and electron microscopes similar?

   _____

   _____

5. How are optical and electron microscopes different?

   _____

   _____

6. What is one important advantage an optical microscope has over a more powerful electron microscope?

   _____

   _____

The Man Who Saved the Children

epidemic: an outbreak of a disease affecting a large number of people

eradicated: got rid of

vaccine: an injection or oral medicine that produces immunity to a disease

immunity: the power of the body to resist infection

placebo: a substance that is given as a medicine even though it has no effect on a disease or infection

The March of Dimes—a charitable organization whose purpose was to fight polio—was founded in 1938 by President Franklin D. Roosevelt. Roosevelt's bout with polio left him unable to use his legs for the rest of his life.

Another scientist, Albert Sabin, developed a polio vaccine a few years after Salk. Sabin's vaccine was given by mouth, and it used a weakened live virus instead of a killed one. Today, it is the most common polio vaccine used around the world.

How did Jonas Salk change the lives of children around the world?

You may never have heard of a disease called *polio*, but there's no doubt your grandparents have. Just half a century ago, polio was an **epidemic**. Parents were afraid to let their children go to swimming pools, the beach, and movie theaters. Schools closed to prevent the spread of the disease. Today, polio has been **eradicated** in the United States.

Polio is a disease that affects the nervous system. The early symptoms can be confused with the flu. In most cases, a person can have polio without even knowing it because the body's immune system fights the disease effectively. Polio moves quickly, though, and when the body can't fight the infection, paralysis and even death can occur.

The first major outbreak of polio in the U.S. happened in 1916. Each following year, nearly 40,000 cases were reported. In the late 1940s, the physician and researcher Jonas Salk began to work on creating a **vaccine** to prevent polio. The common belief at the time was that a person had to be infected by a weak form of the virus in order for the body to build up **immunity** to it. Salk believed that the same effect could be achieved by using the dead virus. It wouldn't make people become ill, but it would produce immunity to the infection in their bodies.

The first large-scale test of the vaccine occurred in 1954. Just two years earlier, a record 58,000 cases of polio had been reported. Salk performed a study with 1.8 million children, who became known as the *Polio Pioneers*. He divided the children into three groups. The first group received the vaccine. The members of the second group were injected with a **placebo**, a substance that wasn't actually a medicine. The third group received neither the vaccine nor the placebo; they were just observed to see how many would contract the disease. The study was double-blind—neither the researchers nor the subjects knew who was receiving the real vaccine until after the data was collected.

Salk and his team of researchers were overjoyed at the results. Salk had been right: a vaccine made of the dead polio virus gave children immunity from the dangerous live virus. Within two years, the number of polio cases dropped nearly 90 percent. By the 1960s, polio had been eradicated in most of the world. Today, there is still no cure for the disease, so immunization remains very important for children everywhere.

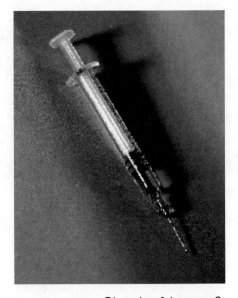

Use the words in the box to complete the sentences below.

eradicated	epidemic	vaccine	immunity

1. A polio _____ occurred in the United States during the 1950s.

2. A vaccine produces _____ to infection.

3. The purpose of a _____ is to prevent disease or infection.

4. Diseases that have been _____ in an area of the world no longer exist there.

Write your answers on the lines below.

5. Why did Salk divide the children in his study into three groups instead of giving the vaccine to all the children?

    _____

    _____

6. Why did the third group of children in Salk's study receive neither the placebo nor the vaccine?

    _____

7. Dr. Linh is performing a test on the effects of a new headache medicine she developed. She gives half her subjects the headache medicine and gives the other half a pill that looks the same but doesn't contain any active ingredients.

    This is an example of using _____.

8. How were the viruses that Sabin used in his polio vaccine different from those used by Salk?

    _____

    _____

What's Next?

Patients given a placebo may feel better because they think they were medically treated. This is known as the *placebo effect*. Do some research to learn more about it. How did scientists figure out what was taking place? What is the purpose of using a placebo in a scientific study?

Review

Circle the letter of the best answer to each question below.

1. How does carbon-14 help scientists determine the age of a fossil?

   a. They know how long it takes half the carbon-14 to change into nitrogen.

   b. They know that carbon-14 only existed during one period in Earth's history.

   c. They put the fossil into a container filled with carbon-14 and observe the reaction.

   d. They know how much carbon-14 collects onto rocks every thousand years.

2. Today, Planet X is better known as which planet?

   a. Neptune

   b. Pluto

   c. Jupiter

   d. Planet X was never found.

3. An electron microscope uses _____ to magnify objects too small to be seen with an optical microscope.

   a. powerful lasers

   b. magnetism

   c. a beam of electrons

   d. All of the above

4. Which of the following is not an important safety rule to follow in the lab?

   a. Never bring food or drinks into the lab.

   b. Wash your hands every five to ten minutes.

   c. Make sure you know how to use all the equipment before you begin.

   d. Never look down into a container that is being heated.

Write your answers on the lines below.

5. When you finish an experiment, why is it dangerous to pour any leftover chemicals down the sink?

   _____

6. Explain why observation always plays a role in experimenting.

   _____

   _____

7. In the yeast experiment, one bottle contained yeast and water. The other bottle contained yeast, water, and sugar. What was the variable in this experiment?

_____

8. How did Ms. Wilson's demonstration with the glass of ice water help Julio solve the mystery of his ruined posters?

_____

9. Paleontologists at the La Brea Tar Pits found fossilized remains of animals of many different sizes, from insects to mastodons. Why was this important?

_____

10. What evidence led Wegener to form his hypothesis about continental drift and Pangaea?

_____

11. What is a placebo?

_____

Use the words in the box to complete the sentences below.

calculations	hypothesis	vacuum	organisms
vaccine	control	observation	molecules

12. _____ are small pieces of matter made up of two or more atoms joined together.

13. The purpose of a _____ is to give the person who receives it immunity to a disease.

14. A _____ group is used to compare how a variable will affect an outcome.

15. Mathematical _____ play an important role in most types of science.

16. When an experiment isn't possible, scientists rely on _____ to make discoveries.

17. Fossils show the remains of _____ that lived during earlier periods in Earth's history.

18. In order to create a _____, air and any other matter must be removed from the space.

19. An experiment should be carefully designed to prove or disprove a _____.

Lesson 2.1 Splitting the Atom

nucleus: the central part of an atom that contains protons and neutrons

ion: an atom with a positive or negative electrical charge

mass: the quantity of matter something has

isotopes: atoms that have more or less neutrons than other atoms of the same element

unstable: ready to break apart, change, or react

radioactive decay: the natural disintegration of an isotope's nucleus

nuclear fission: splitting an atom's nucleus

The more overstuffed an isotope's nucleus is with neutrons, the more readily it will break apart. For this reason, the isotope uranium-235 is commonly used in nuclear reactors.

Isotopes release three different kinds of particles—alpha, beta, or gamma particles. Although they all can cause damage, alpha particles are fairly weak. They cannot get through your skin. Beta particles are strong enough to penetrate your skin. Gamma particles are very dangerous. This form of radiation can cause burns, cancer, or even death.

How do scientists break apart something as small as an atom's nucleus?

Most atoms have the same basic structure. The atom's **nucleus** contains the protons and neutrons, while the electrons buzz around outside it. Protons have positive electrical charges, electrons have negative charges, and neutrons are neutral.

Atoms gain and lose electrons pretty easily—remember, that's what electricity is. When an atom has more or less electrons than protons, it's called an **ion**. Electrons are extremely tiny and have almost no **mass**. Nearly all of an atom's mass is made up by its protons and neutrons.

Sometimes, atoms have extra neutrons inside the nucleus. These atoms are called **isotopes**, and sometimes the extra neutrons make isotopes **unstable**. One common unstable isotope is carbon-14, which has six protons and eight neutrons in its nucleus. It has an atomic weight of 14. A stable carbon atom has an atomic weight of 12—six protons and six neutrons.

Unstable isotopes always try to return to a stable state, without too many extra neutrons. In order to do this, isotopes emit particles of energy to get rid of their extra neutrons. You know this energy better as *radiation*. Isotopes release this energy in a process called **radioactive decay**, which happens at a very steady rate called a *half-life*. The half-life of some isotopes lasts just a few seconds, while other isotopes' half-lives last thousands of years.

In the early 20th century, scientists realized that it might be possible to speed up the process of radioactive decay. What they discovered was that the nucleus of an unstable isotope—already overfilled with neutrons—splits apart instantly if they shoot even more neutrons into it. Then, when the nucleus breaks apart, some of the extra neutrons fly out and smash into the nucleuses of other isotopes nearby. This causes them to split apart as well. A chain reaction begins that releases an incredible amount of energy. If this reaction isn't controlled, it creates a massive explosion.

Splitting an atom's nucleus is called **nuclear fission**. Atomic bombs use nuclear fission to create an uncontrolled chain reaction that explodes with incredible force. Nuclear power plants use nuclear fission, too, but they're carefully designed to control the chain reaction. Instead of a wild explosion, fission creates tremendous amounts of heat that is used to generate electricity.

NAME _____

Circle the letter of the best answer to each question below.

1. Stable atoms have

   a. twice as many neutrons as protons.

   b. the same number of electrons and protons.

   c. a positive electrical charge.

   d. equal numbers of electrons and protons in their nucleuses.

2. What are shot at an isotope's nucleus to trigger a nuclear chain reaction?

   a. gamma particles

   b. electrons

   c. neutrons

   d. ions

Write your answers on the lines below.

3. How are isotopes different from stable atoms?

   _____

4. Uranium is a type of rock. It's most commonly found in Earth's crust as uranium-238. All uranium atoms contain 92 protons. How many neutrons are stuffed into the nucleus of uranium-238?

   _____

5. Explain the difference between nuclear fission in an atomic bomb and in a nuclear reactor.

   _____

   _____

Unifying Concepts and Processes

In the previous chapter, you learned that carbon-14 can be used to determine the age of artifacts that contain that particular isotope. Other isotopes can be used for dating as well. Uranium-235 has a half-life of 704 million years, and uranium-238 has a half-life of 4.6 billion years. What do you think these two isotopes could be used to measure?

Energy on the Move

thermodynamics: the study of energy movement; *thermo* is Greek for "heat" and *dynamics* is Greek for "power"

entropy: disorder; randomness

absolute zero: the temperature (about -459°F) at which no energy exists so atoms and molecules stop moving; this temperature is only a theory and has not been reached

The study of thermodynamics began when people first had the idea of using steam to power engines. They needed to carefully study how energy moved through the engine so they could find out where it was being wasted. Once an efficient steam engine was invented, factories in Europe began using them and the Industrial Revolution began. Steam engines were used to power trains, steamboats, and the first automobiles.

How do the laws of thermodynamics rule the universe?

Thermodynamics is the study of how energy moves through the world. Remember, heat is energy moving from one place to another. When heat adds energy to a substance, the atoms and molecules begin moving more rapidly—they have more thermal energy. The amount of thermal energy in a substance determines whether it will be a solid, liquid, or gas.

The molecules in solids are packed tightly together and move slowly. Heat increases the thermal energy, so the molecules move more rapidly and bounce against each other with more force. They need more room to move, so the solid expands and the substance changes into a liquid. More heat brings more thermal energy, and the substance expands once more to become a gas.

Energy doesn't just flow randomly around the universe, though. It follows the Three Laws of Thermodynamics.

First Law: *Energy is neither created nor destroyed.* This means that there's only so much energy in the universe. It constantly moves around, but the amount never changes. Drop an ice cube into a cup of hot cocoa and you'll see this law in action. Thermal energy moves from the cocoa into the ice, and the solid turns to a liquid—the ice melts. At the same time, the cocoa cools because it lost thermal energy to the ice. On a much bigger scale, energy moves from place to place in the universe, but the total amount never changes.

Second Law: *The natural state of the universe is **entropy**.* When two substances have different amounts of thermal energy, this second law says that the energy will move between them until they both have equal amounts. Heat always flows toward the substance with less thermal energy, though. The only way to get heat to move in the opposite direction is to use more energy.

Third Law: *As a substance approaches **absolute zero**, its entropy becomes total.* At absolute zero, atoms and molecules stop moving. They have no energy because they're spread evenly and randomly throughout the substance. Absolute zero is only a theory, though. Just remember that the colder something is, the less energy it has.

Circle the letter of the best answer to each question below.

1. The energy that a substance contains is

   a. equilibrium.

   b. heat.

   c. thermal energy.

   d. entropy.

2. Energy always moves from

   a. water to ice to gas.

   b. substances with more energy toward those with less.

   c. areas with low energy toward areas with high energy.

   d. equilibrium to entropy.

3. The amount of energy in the universe is

   a. always changing.

   b. being created and destroyed all the time.

   c. always moving toward absolute zero.

   d. constant.

Write your answers on the lines below.

4. In Earth's atmosphere, hot air near the surface always rises toward the cooler air higher in the atmosphere. This is an example of which law of thermodynamics?

   _____

5. When you walk barefoot across a hot sidewalk, you feel the heat on your feet. Explain what's happening with the molecules in both the sidewalk and your feet, and which direction thermal energy is moving.

   _____

   _____

6. When you pick up an ice cube, your hand gets cold. Using the laws of thermodynamics, explain why your hand feels cold.

   _____

   _____

A Shining Example of Clean Energy

greenhouse gases: gases that contribute to the heating of Earth's surface

efficient: done without wasted effort or expense

heat: energy moving from one area to another; it always moves toward the area with less thermal energy

turbine: a rotating engine that works when a gas or liquid flows through it

semiconductors: solid elements that aren't great conductors, but which can be altered by human beings to perform specific electrical tasks, especially in computers; silicon is the most commonly used semiconductor

photons: tiny packets of electromagnetic radiation or energy

The world's largest solar power plant is located in the Mojave Desert in California. More than 900,000 mirrors create intense heat that is used to boil water and make steam. The steam is used to turn a turbine and create electricity.

Why isn't solar power used very often?

Most of the electricity you use every day is created by burning coal. Coal is a fossil fuel, and like all fossil fuels, burning it creates **greenhouse gases**. Alternative energy sources are being used more and more to provide the electricity we need to run our world. Wind power is one of the cleanest options, but solar energy is the most abundant power source we have on the planet. It is also very clean.

Every day, the sun sends an enormous amount of energy to Earth's surface. It's many times more than the amount human beings use each day. Finding an **efficient** way to capture the sun's energy and turn it into a usable form is still a challenge, though.

Energy from the sun travels to Earth in the form of radiation. You feel this energy as **heat**, and you see some of it as visible light.

One use human beings have found for the sun's radiation is to heat things. Mirrors and lenses can be used to focus huge amounts of sunlight onto one small area. All that heat aimed at one spot creates a tremendous amount of thermal energy. It can be used to heat up water or other liquids, which are then used to heat homes. It can also be used to create steam to power a **turbine** and generate electricity.

Another way sunlight can create electricity is through the use of solar cells. These devices, also called *photovoltaic cells*, contain special chemical elements and compounds called **semiconductors**.

Solar cells use **photons** to create electricity. Photons are little packets of energy that all waves of radiation, including sunlight, contain. When the photons in sunlight hit the atoms of a semiconductor, electrons are knocked loose. These loose electrons start traveling among the atoms of the semiconductor. As you know, electricity is electrons on the move. The solar cell captures the electrical energy of these moving electrons and makes it useful for other devices.

There are disadvantages to using solar power. For example, the electricity a solar cell creates is still expensive compared to other methods. Small solar cells are common in calculators, but big electricity users, like office buildings, need a lot of cells to provide enough power. Another disadvantage is that the sun's heat is not available at night and during some storms, so an additional storage device is needed.

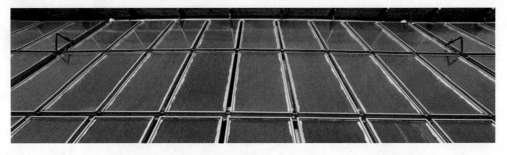

Circle the letter of the best answer to each question below.

1. What is heat?

    a. energy on the move

    b. the opposite of light

    c. the thermal energy stored in matter

    d. a force created by photons

2. A semiconductor is a type of

    a. solar cell.

    b. computer.

    c. chemical.

    d. turbine.

3. Photons are

    a. powerful beams of light.

    b. solar cells used to generate electricity.

    c. packets of electromagnetic energy.

    d. bits of electricity created by a turbine.

Write your answers on the lines below.

4. What is solar radiation?

    _____

5. Explain the difference between using solar cells to create electricity and using mirrors or lenses to create electricity.

    _____

    _____

6. Why haven't solar cells or other forms of solar power replaced the use of fossil fuels?

    _____

7. Do you think solar energy will be used more in the future? Explain your answer.

    _____

inertia: an object's resistance to change in motion unless it is acted upon by an external force

friction: a force that keeps two objects from rubbing smoothly against each other

Isaac Newton was a scientist who lived more than 250 years ago. He may be best remembered for his three laws of motion. Max used Newton's first law of motion, also called the *law of inertia*, to form his hypothesis. The first law states that an object in motion will continue moving at the same speed and in the same direction unless it is acted upon by an outside force. In the same way, an object at rest will stay at rest unless it is acted upon by an outside force.

What role does inertia play in everyday life?

Max and Caleb stood in the driveway, setting up Max's experiment. Max propped up a long wooden board against a plastic storage bin to make a ramp. "Can you put that brick about three feet away from the end of the board?" Max asked his brother.

When everything was in place, Max positioned his skateboard at the edge of the ramp and balanced a small cardboard box on top of it. "You can use the chalk to mark where the box lands when it flies off the skateboard," he told Caleb. Max released the skateboard, and it rolled quickly down the ramp and onto the driveway, where it hit the brick.

The box flew off the skateboard on impact, and Caleb marked the spot where it landed. Max measured the distance and found that the box had traveled 22 inches past the brick.

"How'd you know it would do that?" asked Caleb.

"It's called **inertia**," answered Max. "Inertia is the resistance to change in motion. An object will keep moving at the same speed and in the same direction unless it is acted on by an outside force, like **friction** or gravity."

"Or a brick," said Caleb.

"Exactly," said Max. "Both the skateboard and the box had inertia. The force of the impact with the brick caused the skateboard to stop moving, but the inertia of the box allowed it to continue its movement."

"Why did the box eventually stop moving, even though it didn't hit anything?" asked Caleb.

"The pull of gravity and friction with air molecules and the ground finally made it stop," responded Max.

"We proved your hypothesis, so the experiment was a success, right?" asked Caleb.

Max laughed. "You can be my assistant anytime," he replied.

NAME _____

Write your answers on the lines below.

1. Use Newton's first law of motion to explain why wearing a seat belt in a car can save your life.

_____

_____

_____

2. Describe an everyday situation in which inertia plays a role.

_____

_____

_____

3. The first time Max and Caleb performed the experiment, they placed a plastic cup on the skateboard instead of the small box. When the cup flew off the skateboard, Caleb was not able to mark exactly where it landed. Why wasn't the cup a good choice of material for this experiment?

_____

_____

_____

4. What was Max's hypothesis?

_____

_____

_____

What's Next?

Try this simple experiment at home to see inertia in action. Take an uncooked egg and set it on the counter on its side. Spin the egg and then gently place your fingers on it to stop it. The moment it stops, remove your hand. The egg will begin spinning again. Do you know why? Even though you stopped the motion of the egg's shell, the liquid contents continued to move. What do you think would happen if you tried the same experiment with a hard-boiled egg?

atomic: of or related to the subject of atoms

discharged: let go or got rid of

current: a stream of electrical charges

You're probably most familiar with the shock of static being discharged all at once, but a material with extra electrons naturally loses them over time anyway. When the electrons don't rush out in a single burst, they slowly move out into the air or other surrounding matter.

Static is most noticeable in the winter because the air is so dry. Remember, water is a great conductor. The humid summer air takes away the extra electrons that give a material its static charge.

What makes static electricity different from electricity that flows through wires?

As clothing tumbles around inside a dryer, the different materials rub against each other over and over again. You can't see it, but this friction is causing changes at the **atomic** level inside each piece of clothing. The atoms of some materials, like wool, are losing electrons. Other materials, like nylon or polyester, are gaining electrons in their atoms. You know what happens when atoms gain or lose electrons—they end up with electrical charges.

When the dryer buzzes and you remove the clothes, they snap and pop as you pull them apart. A wool sock that lost electrons ends up with a positive charge, so it sticks to a pair of nylon pants that gained electrons. Remember, opposite charges are attracted to each other, and like charges repel. The different materials want to stick together because of all those electrically charged atoms. The clothes are filled with static electricity.

The word *static* means "unchanging or unmoving." Static electricity is the electrical charges that build up in a material but don't have anywhere to go. When you shuffle across carpeting, your body picks up extra electrons and becomes filled with static electricity. If you touch a good conductor, like metal, the extra electrons are **discharged** all at once, and you feel the force of them leaving your body as a tiny shock.

A simple experiment can show you how static electricity is different than the electricity flowing through wires and bringing power to your home.

First, you need to gather the materials. Find a hard rubber comb and a fluorescent light bulb—an incandescent bulb with a wire filament inside won't work. Then, you need a dark place to perform the experiment, like a closet. It also wouldn't hurt to wear a wool sweater, but if your hair is nice and dry, you should be okay.

Once you've shut yourself into the closet, rub the comb against your sweater or run it through your hair. Do it a few times to be sure plenty of extra electrons move into the comb to build up enough static electricity. Then, carefully touch the comb to the bulb's glass surface. You should see sparks lighting up the fluorescent gas inside the bulb.

The electrical **current** flowing from a socket is much bigger and more powerful than the static electricity in the comb. But there's only one kind of electricity—electrons moving from atom to atom.

Circle the letter of the best answer to each question below.

1. The fluorescent gas lit up because _____ flowed from the comb into the bulb.

   a. static electricity

   b. electrons

   c. an electrical current

   d. Both b and c

2. A material with extra electrons will often stick to a material with missing electrons because

   a. the electrons fit together like puzzle pieces.

   b. positive charges are attracted to negative charges.

   c. positive charges are repelled by negative charges.

   d. the electrical charges create a vacuum that holds the materials together.

Write your answers on the lines below.

3. When your body fills with extra electrons and you touch a good conductor, you get a shock. Is this shock an example of static electricity or an electrical current? Explain your answer. (Hint: Review the definitions of *static* and *current*.)

   _____

   _____

4. Why is static more noticeable in the winter than in the summer?

   _____

   _____

What's Next?

Try experimenting with different materials to see which ones are most likely to gain extra electrons. You know that hair and wool easily give up electrons, so use them to pass extra electrons to the materials you want to test. Try testing a balloon, a glass jar, a metal bowl, and a piece of newspaper. Use a hole punch to create tiny bits of paper. If a material has a static charge, the bits of paper should stick to it. Which materials collected plenty of electrons? Which ones didn't?

Taking to the Skies

drag: a force that works against an object in motion

lift: a force that causes a bird to rise in the air

thrust: a force that pushes an object forward through the air

Both birds and airplanes need an energy source. Planes use fuel and engines. Birds have strong wing and chest muscles that allow them to propel themselves by flapping. They use a great deal of energy in flight and must eat a lot to keep up their supply.

Large birds, like vultures and eagles, can stay in the air for hours at a time. They save energy by soaring instead of flapping. They do this by riding rising columns of warm air called *thermals*. When they reach a certain height, they move out of the thermal and glide, letting the wind carry them to the next thermal.

How do birds stay in the air?

A hawk soars through the air on a warm spring day. A robin swoops from a branch to a puddle on the ground. Before human beings found a way to fly, they spent much time observing the flight of birds. It took them years to uncover the secrets that allow birds to move through the air so quickly and efficiently.

In order to fly, a bird must overcome two forces—gravity and **drag**. You probably already know that gravity is the force that pulls objects toward Earth. If you are holding a book and release it, gravity causes the book to fall. Drag, or resistance, is a force that works against an object in motion. The next time you're in a pool, quickly move your hand through the water. The force of the water that pushes against your hand as you move it is drag.

When a bird takes flight, it must rise upward (overcoming gravity) and move forward (overcoming drag). **Lift**—the force that allows a bird to rise into the air—is caused by a difference in air pressure. When a bird flaps its wings, air rushes over and under them. Because of the curved shape of the wing, the air flowing over the top surface moves more quickly than the air below it. This creates a difference in air pressure; it's lower above the wing and higher below. These differences in air pressure push up on the wing and produce lift.

As the bird flaps its wings, it creates **thrust**, which propels the bird forward. If it flapped its wings in a straight up-and-down motion, it would hover in place. Instead, a bird pushes itself forward on the downstroke. On the upstroke, the wings are angled so that less of their surface comes in contact with the air. In a way, it's similar to rowing a boat. You use the oar to push the water away from you. Then, you must lift the oar from the water to bring it back to its starting position before you can begin the next stroke.

The bones of birds are hollow and light, which makes flight easier. Birds' feathers also help them fly. Contour feathers give birds their sleek, streamlined shape that allows them to move easily through the air. Flight feathers are shaped to provide lift and to help the bird steer. A bird's body is perfectly suited to flight—something human beings can imitate.

Use the words in the box to complete the sentences below.

food	lift	air pressure	muscles	feathers	thrust	thermals

1. _____ and _____ are the two forces that a bird needs in order to fly.

2. A difference in _____ produces lift.

3. Some birds ride _____, which are columns of warm, rising air.

4. Planes use engines and fuel as energy sources, whereas birds use _____ and

    _____.

5. The shape of a bird's wings and _____ help it fly.

Write your answers on the lines below.

6. How are the bones of birds different from other animals?

    _____

7. Why does soaring allow a bird to conserve energy?

    _____

8. What is the difference between lift and thrust?

    _____

    _____

9. Explain how the motion of a bird's flapping wings propel it forward.

    _____

    _____

What's Next?

Do some research to learn more about how airplanes fly. How is the flight of a plane similar to the flight of a bird? How are they different?

potential energy: stored energy that is created by the force of gravity; for example, a rock on a hill has potential energy

kinetic energy: the energy of motion; if the rock begins rolling downhill, its potential energy will have changed into kinetic energy

conservation of energy: energy is neither created nor destroyed, it just changes forms; this is the First Law of Thermodynamics

oscillation: one complete swing back and forth

Galileo's work with pendulums was just one part of his larger study of gravity. Galileo's experiments showed that an object's weight has no effect on how quickly it falls. In other words, Earth's gravity pulls on all objects with an equal force. A boulder will fall at the same speed as a penny.

How is the swing of a pendulum affected by weight and distance?

A pendulum is an extremely simple device—a weight hanging from a string swings back and forth. Around 1600, the Italian physicist Galileo Galilei discovered some amazing facts about pendulums. Alexis and Miranda want to test a few of Galileo's findings.

First, Alexis hangs a small lead weight from an 18-inch string. She attaches the other end to a metal bar. Miranda places a chair about a foot away from the pendulum so the girls can use the chair's back as a marker.

Alexis pulls the weight back until it's touching the wood, and then she releases it. The weight swings away and then back toward the chair. It returns to almost the exact place where it began, pausing just a millimeter or two shy of the chair's back before it begins the next swing.

Miranda writes in her notebook, "When we pulled the weight back, it had **potential energy** because of gravity. When we released the weight, its potential energy changed into **kinetic energy**. There was enough kinetic energy to carry the weight back to almost the exact place where it began. It had nearly the same amount of potential energy at the end of the swing as it did at the beginning. This is an example of the **conservation of energy**."

Miranda pulls the weight back and releases it again. Alexis times how long it takes for the pendulum to make one complete swing back and forth. Then, Miranda pulls the weight back twice as far and releases it. Alexis times the swing again, and the girls are surprised to find that the amount of time is the same. After trying several different distances, the girls conclude that one **oscillation** always takes the same amount of time.

Miranda writes, "As long as we used the same weight, the amount of time this pendulum took to complete one swing didn't change even when the distance of the swing changed. This means the speed must be changing—the farther the pendulum swings, the faster it moves."

Next, the girls use different weights. They attach a second 18-inch string to the bar and use cork for the weight. Alexis pulls both weights back the same distance and lets them go. The girls count the number of swings each weight made in ten seconds. The numbers are equal.

"Weight doesn't affect the speed of the pendulum. In ten seconds, both weights swing the same number of times."

Circle the letter of the best answer to each question below.

1. As a pendulum swings back and forth, each oscillation is a tiny bit shorter than the one before it. What is happening with the speed of each swing?

    a. Each swing is faster than the one before it.

    b. Each swing is slower than the one before it.

    c. The speed of the swings remains constant.

    d. The swings speed up and slow down randomly.

2. Which experiment proved that gravity pulls with the same force on all objects?

    a. the girls' first experiment (conservation of energy)

    b. the girls' second experiment (the effect of distance on swing speed)

    c. the girls' third experiment (the effect of weight on swing speed)

    d. none of the girls' experiments

Write your answers on the lines below.

3. The weight pauses for a split second each time it reaches the high point of its swing. At that moment, does the weight have potential or kinetic energy? Explain your answer.

    _____

4. According to the conservation of energy, a pendulum should swing forever as the energy keeps changing from potential to kinetic and back again. This might happen inside a vacuum, but in Earth's atmosphere, the weight loses a little bit of energy with each swing. What's causing the energy loss, and where is the energy going?

    _____

    _____

What's Next?

What effect does the length of the string have on a pendulum's swing? Create your own pendulum with string and a small weight and then count the number of swings it makes in fifteen seconds. Shorten the string by half and try again. Be sure not to introduce too many variables or the experiment won't work. Keep the weight the same, as well the distance you pull the weight back.

Boyle's Perfect Mixtures

alchemy: the ancient art of experimenting with metals

analysis: studying something by breaking it down into smaller parts

elements: substances that can't be broken down; each element contains only one kind of atom

mixtures: combinations of two or more substances that haven't become chemically bound together

compounds: two or more substances that have combined together chemically to form a new substance

chemical bond: the force that holds atoms together in order to form molecules

chemical reaction: a process that breaks chemical bonds or forms new ones

Boyle's Law is a famous math equation about the relationship between air pressure and volume. Boyle used it to study Earth's atmosphere and what keeps our air from floating out into space.

Why is Robert Boyle sometimes called the Father of Chemistry?

British scientist Robert Boyle was born in 1627 into a very wealthy family. He didn't need to worry about making a living, so he could spend his time experimenting and writing books.

The 1600s were an important time for science and math in England. Boyle lived near Oxford, where many of the greatest scientists of that time were working. He even knew Sir Isaac Newton.

Boyle was a pioneer in changing **alchemy** into modern chemistry. Alchemy was an ancient way of experimenting with metals. Although some alchemists discovered important things, most of them spent their time on impossible tasks, such as trying to turn ordinary metal into gold.

Boyle took the science of his day to a new level. He was one of the first scientists to carefully record all the results of his experiments. He also insisted that chemistry should focus on **analysis**—the study of what substances are made of. This specific goal marked the change of alchemy into what we know today as modern chemistry.

Boyle analyzed many different substances, which led later scientists to define the **elements** as those substances that can't be broken down any further. Boyle's greatest work, though, might have been in seeing the difference between **mixtures** and **compounds**.

Mixtures and compounds are both ways of combining substances, but the atoms and molecules in mixtures and compounds do different things. For example, air is a mixture. Oxygen, nitrogen, and other elements float around together, but they aren't connected chemically. You can easily separate the elements that are found in air.

Compounds are different. Boyle called them "perfectly mixed" because they aren't easily separated into the different elements they contain. Water is a compound of hydrogen and oxygen. Its chemical symbol, H_2O, tells you that each molecule contains two hydrogen atoms connected to one oxygen atom. These three atoms have a **chemical bond** with each other, meaning they can only be separated by a **chemical reaction**.

Boyle's discoveries about mixtures and compounds opened the door for other scientists to discover molecules, atoms, and the rest of modern chemistry.

Circle the letter of the best answer to each question below.

1. Boyle used analysis to study

   a. substances.

   b. molecules.

   c. alchemy.

   d. All of the above

2. H_2O is water's chemical symbol. This symbol tells you that

   a. water is a mixture.

   b. water contains the elements hydrogen and oxygen.

   c. each water molecule contains a total of two atoms.

   d. each water molecule has two oxygen atoms.

Write your answers on the lines below.

3. What do mixtures and compounds have in common?

   _____

4. How is a compound different from a mixture?

   _____

   _____

5. Table salt is sodium chloride, or NaCl. Is table salt a mixture or a compound?

   _____

6. Explain how alchemy and chemistry are related.

   _____

   _____

Unifying Concepts and Processes

Energy is needed to break chemical bonds. Using this piece of information, what role does heat play in a chemical reaction?

_____

_____

Acid or Base?

concentration: the amount of something in a substance

neutral: neither an acid nor a base

acid: a sour substance that has a pH of less than 7

base: a bitter substance that has a pH of greater than 7

pH indicator: a chemical that changes color when it comes in contact with an acid or a base

A few plants, like pine trees, azaleas, blueberries, and tomatoes, grow better in acidic than neutral soil. If the soil is too acidic, though, bacteria may not be able to live in it. This is a problem because bacteria are needed to break down materials and make nutrients available to plants.

Normal rain has a pH of about 5.6. It is more acidic than pure water because carbon dioxide in the air forms a weak acid with it. Acid rain, a result of pollution, has a pH of about 4.3.

How can you tell whether the soil in your yard can support a certain type of plant?

If anyone in your family likes to garden, you may have heard them mention something called *pH*. Gardeners, as well as scientists, use this scale of measurement to determine how acidic something is. Garden centers sell pH kits so that you can test the soil in your yard. Knowing the pH of your soil can help you choose plants that are likely to grow well and thrive.

The pH scale measures the **concentration** of hydrogen ions in a substance. The scale runs from 0 to 14. Pure water is in the middle of the scale with a pH of 7, which means that it is **neutral**. A substance that is neutral is neither an **acid** nor a **base**. Substances that measure below 7 on the scale are acids, and those that measure above 7 are alkaline, or basic. For example, lemon juice, which is very acidic, has a pH of 2. Ammonia, a household cleaner, is basic and has a pH of 11.

The measure between units on the pH scale is different than it is on other types of scales. Each unit represents a tenfold change, or a change by the power of 10. Something that has a pH of 4 has 10 times more hydrogen than something with a pH of 5. A substance that has a pH of 3 has 100 (10 x 10) times more hydrogen than a substance with a pH of 5.

A substance's pH can be measured using a **pH indicator**, such as a strip of litmus paper. If you dip the litmus paper in a liquid, like bleach or vinegar, it will change color. By comparing the color of the paper with the colors on the pH scale, you can tell whether something is an acid or a base. The colors on the pH scale appear in the same order as the colors of the rainbow. Acids are on the red end, bases are on the purple end, and neutral materials are green.

Most plants need soil that is neutral or close to neutral, with a pH between 6 and 7. When a gardener doesn't have the right type of soil, he or she can change the acidity. If the soil is too basic, a substance called *sulfate* can be added to it to make it more acidic. Lime, a substance made of calcium oxide, can be added to a soil that is too acidic to boost its pH level.

NAME _____

Circle the letter of the best answer to each question below.

1. A pH indicator measures the concentration of _____ a substance contains.

    a. oxygen atoms

    b. nitrogen isotopes

    c. hydrogen ions

    d. alkaline isotopes

2. Bleach has a pH of 13. Ammonia has a pH of 11. Ammonia contains _____ times as much hydrogen ions as bleach.

    a. 10

    b. 100

    c. 1,000

    d. 10,000

3. The higher a substance's pH, the _____ it is.

    a. more basic

    b. more acidic

    c. closer to neutral

    d. Both a and c

Write your answers on the lines below.

4. Imagine that you have taken a sample of water from a nearby lake. You do a test and find that it has a pH of 5.6. Adding about $\frac{1}{8}$ of a teaspoon of baking soda to it neutralizes it. What does this tell you about the baking soda?

    _____

5. What is one reason that plants cannot survive in soil that is very acidic?

    _____

6. When you dip a litmus strip in a glass of tomato juice, it turns orange. This tells you that the juice is

    _____, and it has a pH of _____ than seven.

7. How is the pH scale different from other scales of measurement, like the Fahrenheit temperature scale?

    _____

Review

Circle the letter of the best answer to each question below.

1. The Second Law of Thermodynamics says that the universe naturally moves toward

   a. high temperatures.

   b. entropy.

   c. solidity.

   d. the areas of highest pressure.

2. The weight of a pendulum is pulled back and released. As it swings back and forth, each complete swing is slightly shorter than the one before it. Although the distance of each swing decreases, the amount of time each swing takes remains the same. Which sentence below correctly describes the weight's inertia?

   a. The first swing has more inertia than the final swing.

   b. The first swing has less inertia than the final swing

   c. The first and final swings have equal amounts of inertia.

   d. The weight does not have any inertia until it has stopped moving.

Write your answers on the lines below.

3. An ion is an atom that has an electrical charge because it gained or lost electrons. What is an isotope?

   _____

4. When an atom's nucleus is split during nuclear fission, a chain reaction can occur that causes nucleuses in nearby atoms to split, too. How is this chain reaction different in nuclear power plants versus nuclear bombs?

   _____

   _____

5. What effect does heat have on the atoms and molecules in matter?

   _____

   _____

6. Why are human beings searching for alternatives to fossil fuels?

   _____

   _____

7. Describe one way that sunlight can be turned into electricity.

_____

8. Explain the difference between static electricity and an electrical current.

_____

9. Use inertia to explain the action of throwing a ball.

_____

10. Explain the similarity between friction and drag.

_____

11. A bowling ball and a golf ball are hung from strings of equal length. If the weights are pulled back the exact same distance and released, which ball will swing the fastest, or will they swing at the same speed?

_____

12. Explain why the air in Earth's atmosphere is a mixture, not a compound.

_____

13. What does the pH scale measure?

_____

Underline the correct answer from the two choices you are given.

14. Atoms always try to return to a (balanced, unbalanced) state.

15. (Thermodynamics, Electromagnetism) is the study of how energy moves through the universe.

16. (Solar cells, Photons) are packets of energy in light.

17. Opposite charges (attract, repel) each other.

18. When the weight of a pendulum is in motion, it has (potential, kinetic) energy.

19. A propeller pulling an airplane through the air is an example of (lift, thrust).

20. A substance that is made up of molecules is a (mixture, compound) of at least two different elements chemically combined.

21. A substance that is neither an acid nor a base is (neutral, concentrated).

Lesson 3.1 Communities of Life

evolved: developed or changed over time

specialized: having one particular task or purpose

contract: squeeze together or become smaller

organelles: the structures inside a cell that do certain tasks

nucleus: the organelle that is in charge of reproduction and makes proteins

membrane: a soft, flexible layer; a cell membrane allows some fluids and solids to pass through it

Your body began as a single cell that divided into two cells. Those two cells divided into four, then eight, sixteen, and so on. After a series of just twenty doublings in this manner, your body had more than one million cells.

Nearly a trillion cells die inside a human body each day.

What do all organisms have in common?

All living organisms are made of cells. Trees, mushrooms, mammals, or insects—they're all alive because cells are doing the work necessary to keep them living. Cells are the building blocks of life.

In a way, every plant and animal is a thriving community of individual living cells. Just like Earth's largest organisms, each cell is born, lives its life, and dies. Cells digest food, use oxygen, produce waste, and have the ability to reproduce. In fact, the first life forms to appear on Earth were individual cells floating in the prehistoric oceans. Eventually, these cells began working together as groups instead of alone, and Earth's organisms became bigger and more complex.

Earth still has plenty of single-celled organisms—bacteria, for example—but the plants and animals you are most familiar with contain trillions of cells. The cells aren't all exactly the same, though. Cells **evolved** to perform **specialized** tasks inside each organism.

The human body contains trillions of cells, but they can be divided into a couple of hundred different categories based on their functions. For example, red blood cells carry oxygen to the other cells in the body. Neurons carry electrical messages back and forth between the brain and other areas. Muscle cells have the ability to **contract**, which gives the body movement.

Like the organs inside your body, plant and animal cells contain tiny **organelles** that help them digest food, remove waste, and perform the other tasks that keep them alive. The most important organelle is the **nucleus**. It's like the cell's brain, and it controls what happens inside the cell. It also contains the information necessary to make another copy of the cell. The nucleus allows the cell to reproduce, which it needs to do to grow.

Plant and animal cells are similar, but there are two big differences between them. First, animal cells are enclosed in a soft cell **membrane** that allows them to take many different shapes. Plants have a soft cell membrane, too, but it's surrounded by a stiff cell wall. This wall supports and protects the cell inside it.

Plant cells also contain plastids, which aren't found in animal cells. Plastids are organelles that contain chlorophyll, which helps the cell produce food during photosynthesis and gives plants their green color.

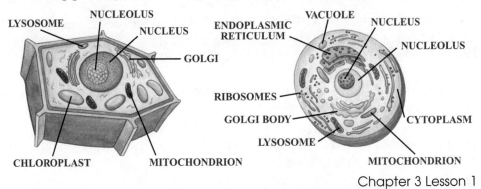

LYSOSOME • NUCLEOLUS • NUCLEUS • GOLGI • CHLOROPLAST • MITOCHONDRION

ENDOPLASMIC RETICULUM • VACUOLE • NUCLEUS • NUCLEOLUS • RIBOSOMES • GOLGI BODY • LYSOSOME • CYTOPLASM • MITOCHONDRION

Circle the letter of the best answer to each question below.

1. Single-celled organisms

   a. were the first life forms on the planet.

   b. became extinct soon after more complex organisms evolved.

   c. can't exist on Earth unless they are parts of large groups.

   d. All of the above

2. The author compares a cell's nucleus to what organ in the human body?

   a. heart

   b. red blood cells

   c. brain

   d. lungs

3. Which of the following statements is not true?

   a. The human body contains trillions of cells.

   b. The cells that make up an organism must compete to survive.

   c. Each human being began as a single cell.

   d. Cells inside your body are living, reproducing, and dying all the time.

Write your answers on the lines below.

4. Give one example of a specific type of cell in the human body.

   _____

5. How are plant cells and animal cells similar?

   _____

6. How are plant cells and animal cells different?

   _____

What's Next?

The illustration on the previous page shows many of the different organelles that can be found in both plant and animal cells. Do some research to identify the different functions each organelle performs in a cell.

Darwin's Finches

species: a classification for grouping organisms that are similar to one another

drought: a time of little or no rain

natural selection: the process by which traits that are best suited to an organism's environment are more likely to be represented in future generations.

"It is not the strongest of the species that survives, nor the most intelligent; it is the one that is the most adaptable to change."—Charles Darwin, naturalist

The Galápagos Islands are famous for having large numbers of plant and animal life that exist nowhere else in the world. For this reason, the islands are a popular place for scientists to conduct research.

Why were the beaks of birds living on the Galápagos Islands worth studying?

In the middle of the Pacific Ocean, near the equator and west of Ecuador, lie the Galápagos Islands. These volcanic islands are the site of studies done by the scientist Charles Darwin. His research there led to the creation of his most well-known theories.

Finches, small, sparrow-like birds, live on the islands. With the help of a colleague, Darwin learned that there were 13 different **species** of finches on the islands. The birds were all about the same size, and they had similar coloring. The main difference that Darwin noticed was in the birds' beaks.

Darwin came to the conclusion that all these different species of finches had an ancestor in common. He believed that over time, they developed different types of beaks to suit different needs. Some had beaks that were suited for crushing, which would be useful for eating seeds. Others had grasping beaks that could hold twigs or thorns and use them as a tool to pull insects from tree branches.

Even though the Galápagos finches have beaks that allow them to eat special foods, their general eating habits don't vary that much from species to species. Instead, they are able to survive difficult times—such as times of **drought** or intense competition—because of their specialized beaks.

Darwin's study of the finches led to his theory of **natural selection**. He believed that certain traits in a species make it better able to survive. Over time and many generations, the traits that benefit the animal become more common. For example, a certain type of coloring in a moth might protect it from predators. According to Darwin, future generations of the moth would have this coloring because it helps the species survive.

In recent years, scientists have watched an example of this theory unfold. Traits usually evolve over a long period of time. In just about 20 years, though, one of Darwin's finches developed a smaller beak so that it could eat smaller seeds. In the past, it fed on seeds of different sizes. Then, another species of finch came to the island and began eating all the larger seeds. A drought also caused greater competition for the existing food. The finches that had smaller beaks were better able to survive these changes. It was a perfect illustration of Darwin's theory of natural selection—in the very same place he had originally formed his theory.

NAME _____

Circle the letter of the best answer to each question below.

1. After observing the many species of finches, Darwin came to believe that they

    a. could not live anywhere outside of the Galápagos Islands.

    b. ate exactly the same foods.

    c. had the same type of beak.

    d. shared a common ancestor.

2. Beak differences among the finches were a result of

    a. natural selection.

    b. differences in diet.

    c. breeding with another species of bird.

    d. Both a and b

Write your answers on the lines below.

3. What makes the Galápagos Islands a unique place to do research?

    _____

    _____

4. What caused one of Darwin's finches to develop a smaller beak in recent years?

    _____

    _____

5. Before the Industrial Revolution took place in England, the gypsy moth was light gray. The factories produced a lot of pollution, and the bark on the trees in the moths' habitat became dark gray. The gypsy moth could no longer camouflage itself. Use your knowledge of natural selection to explain how you think the gypsy moth evolved.

    _____

    _____

    _____

sequence: the order in which things appear or happen

genes: the stretches of DNA molecules that carry the code for proteins. These determine the characteristics or traits a plant, animal, or human being will have

chromosomes: the long molecules of DNA; human beings have 23 pairs of chromosomes

genome: the entire genetic sequence contained in a cell's DNA and chromosomes; the word is a combination of *gene* and *chromosome*

The only people who share the same DNA are identical twins. This is because both siblings developed from the same single fertilized egg cell.

Other than identical twins, every human being has a completely unique chemical sequence in his or her DNA. This is why DNA is helpful to law enforcement.

Chimpanzees—our closest relatives in the animal kingdom—share 96 percent of the their genes with human beings.

Why can DNA be used to identify specific people?

The cells inside your body are smart. They know just what job they're supposed to perform—a blood cell never gets confused and starts acting like a muscle cell. Cells also know when they need to make copies of themselves. They even know when they're supposed to die because they're no longer needed. A special chemical called *DNA* guides them.

DNA stands for **d**eoxyribo**n**ucleic **a**cid. It's found inside every nucleus in every cell in your body. DNA usually looks like long strands of hair bunched up inside the nucleus. For much of a cell's life, DNA is busy telling the cell to make special chemicals. There proteins are needed for every job and process that goes on in that type of cell. When it's time for the cell to reproduce, then DNA has the specific job of making a copy of itself.

Up close, each piece of DNA looks like a long, twisted ladder. Each side of the ladder contains a **sequence** of chemicals. At each rung, the chemical on one side combines with a chemical on the other side. DNA uses only four chemicals, but a huge number of combinations are possible in each strand.

Genes are stretches of the DNA molecule that have a specific combination of these four chemicals. Your genes contain all the information that your cells need to make you the person that you are. Your genes have the code for making all of your body systems, organs, and cells. They also can be unique from person to person, telling what color your eyes are, for example.

DNA is found as a very long molecule called a *chromosome*. Human beings have 23 pairs of identical **chromosomes** inside each nucleus, making a total of 46 chromosomes. When the cell divides, the pairs are split up, and each half gets 23 unique chromosomes. Before a cell can divide again, it has to create more DNA in order to have 23 pairs again.

As a group, the chromosomes are called a **genome**. The human genome contains about 35,000 genes. Each person has basically the same genome with unique variations, and every cell in his or her body contains this unique genome. It's hard to believe, but this means that every single cell holds all the information to make an exact copy of the individual it's a part of.

Remember, organisms begin as single cells that divide over and over again. The DNA that was in that first cell's nucleus got copied each time the cells divided. In the end, every cell in an organism contains all the genetic information necessary to make the entire organism again.

Circle the letter of the best answer to each question below.

1. Where is DNA found?

    a. inside a cell's nucleus

    b. outside a cell's nucleus

    c. outside of a cell

    d. between the layers of a cell's membrane

2. DNA is shaped like a twisted ladder. What occurs at each rung in the ladder?

    a. Chromosomes are formed.

    b. Two chemicals are connected.

    c. DNA is divided into several genes.

    d. A genome is created.

3. The stretches of DNA that have a code for specific information are called

    a. heredity.

    b. chromosome pairs.

    c. genes.

    d. acids.

Write your answers on the lines below.

4. The long molecules of DNA that are usually found in pairs are called _____.

5. The title of this selection compares DNA to a blueprint. Blueprints are drawings that show how a building should be constructed. Explain why DNA is like a blueprint.

    _____

    _____

6. Cloning is the process of making an exact copy of an organism. In order to make a clone, a scientist needs only one cell from the organism he or she is going to clone. Why?

    _____

    _____

Blowing in the Wind

spores: cells that can grow into new organisms, like ferns or mushrooms

fungi: a large group of plant-like organisms that include mushrooms, mold, and yeast; fungi digest their food outside themselves and then absorb the nutrients

lichens: combinations of fungi and seaweed-related plants called an *algae*

Tropical tree ferns can grow to be 80 feet tall. They look more like palm trees than the ferns people keep as houseplants.

A giant puffball mushroom releases about seven trillion spores.

Most of a mushroom grows underground. It sprouts a mushroom stem and cap only to produce spores out of the gills under the cap. Scientists have found an underground mushroom in Oregon that covers 2,200 acres, or an area of about 3.5 square miles. The giant fungus is thought to be at least 2,400 years old.

How did that colorful life form grow in your fridge?

Picture the world 380 million years ago. It was a time long before dinosaurs, when the only living land creatures were insects. Skinny tree trunks reached more than 30 feet into the air. Green leaves grew from the treetops, shading the woods like hundreds of green umbrellas. No plants with seeds existed yet, so how could the trees reproduce? Tiny **spores** drifted from the tree leaves, down to the rich forest floor below.

Spores are living cells that are transported away from the parent plant by wind, water, or insects. Like all cells, they carry genetic information. They are often too small to see, but a large group can look like dust or smoke. Spores are strong cells because they can resist harsh conditions, such as heat, cold, or lack of water. When the environment is right, they start to grow into a new plant. Plants that reproduce with spores include mosses, **fungi**, **lichens**, and ferns.

When that old bread you forgot in the back of the fridge grows mold on it, it first looks like a white web. The white part is actually made of many tiny stalks. After a while, small black or green spore cases grow on top of the stalks. Black mold is more common on starchy foods, like bread, while green mold tends to grow on fruits and vegetables. When the spore cases open, they spew out millions of new spores, which allows the mold to grow and spread.

Most of the time, we think of mold as something unwanted and unpleasant. Certain types of mold can even be dangerous if they are inhaled. Other molds can be useful. For example, they can be used to create flavorful cheeses, like blue cheese, gorgonzola, and brie. You may have even taken a medicine, like penicillin, that was made from mold.

Many spore-produced organisms, like mushrooms, mosses, and ferns, have alternating generations. Every other generation produces spores, but the middle generation is different. For example, you might have noticed round bumps on the bottoms of fern leaves. These bumps are spore cases. When they dry out, they drop thousands of spores on the ground. When conditions are right, a small, flat, heart-shaped plant grows out of the spores. This is the middle generation, or the parent. A tiny fern, which resembles the grandparent plant, grows from the parent, and the parent dies. Someday, the tiny fern will have spore cases on its leaves, and the cycle will continue.

Circle the letter of the best answer to the question below.

1. Which of the following is not likely to be a form of transportation for spores?

   a. a gust of wind

   b. a rainstorm

   c. a pebble in a garden

   d. an ant crawling along the forest floor

Underline the correct answer from the two choices you are given.

2. A mushroom is a type of (spore, fungus).

3. Spores are how some organisms (reproduce, move).

4. Organisms like ferns and fungi have alternating (generations, cycles).

5. (Lichen, Mold) grows on food that has begun to decay.

Write your answers on the lines below.

6. What are two ways in which some types of mold are useful to human beings?

   _____

7. How is a parent generation of a fern different from the generation that comes before and after it?

   _____

   _____

8. Plants that reproduced using _____ existed before seed-bearing plants did.

9. How are spores similar to seeds?

   _____

10. Why do parts of a mushroom become visible above ground?

    _____

11. How are organisms that have alternating generations different from most plants and animals?

    _____

converted: changed from one form into another

nitrogen cycle: the cycle that shows the movement of nitrogen between the air, plants, soil, and animals on Earth

fertilizers: manure or chemicals used on plants or crops to improve their growth and health

irrigate: to artificially supply land or crops with water

Some of the nitrogen found in soil has an unusual source. Lightning changes free nitrogen in the air into a compound called *nitric dioxide*. It dissolves in water and makes its way into the soil during a rain shower.

When bodies of water contain large amounts of nitrates, lots of algae grow. Algae use up a lot of oxygen in the water, which can cause other organisms to die.

What role do bacteria play in making nitrogen useful for all living things?

Take a deep breath. What did you just inhale? You know that your body needs oxygen to function, so you must have inhaled oxygen. That's true, but the air you breathe is only about 21% oxygen. Earth's atmosphere is also made up of 78% nitrogen. All living things need nitrogen to grow and develop, but they can't use free nitrogen, which is the form found in the atmosphere. The nitrogen needs to be **converted** to a form that plants and animals can use.

Certain types of bacteria are the only living creatures that can use free nitrogen. They take nitrogen from the air and soil, where it is found in animal waste and decaying plant and animal material. The bacteria "fix" it, or change it into a usable form. Ammonia, nitrates, and nitrites are nitrogen compounds that plants can absorb. By converting free nitrogen to these compounds, the nitrogen-fixing bacteria provide plants with exactly what they need to grow.

Animals get their nitrogen by eating plants or by eating herbivores—animals that consume plants. All animals produce waste, which contains free nitrogen. The waste makes its way back into the soil. Eventually, the animals and plants die. More free nitrogen is returned to the soil from the decayed plants and animals, and the **nitrogen cycle** continues.

Balance is important in nature. Imagine a giant seesaw. When weight is placed on one end, the other end rises. In nature, basic processes and cycles usually work to bring the seesaw back to a level position, or equilibrium. Because plants and animals are constantly using nitrogen, it must also be returned to the atmosphere to maintain the natural balance.

That's the role that denitrifying bacteria play. They turn the nitrogen compounds in the soil back into gas that is released into the air. In a way, they perform a job that is opposite of the nitrogen-fixing bacteria. Together, they help balance the level of nitrogen in the soil and the atmosphere.

Human beings have upset this balance by using too many **fertilizers** that contain nitrates. Rain water and water used to **irrigate** crops can carry these nitrates to rivers and lakes. This occurs before bacteria have a chance to convert the nitrates back into nitrogen gas. Too many nitrates in the water can make it dangerous for people and animals to use—just another reason for human beings to be careful of how their actions affect the natural world.

Write **true** or **false** next to each statement below.

1. _____ Both lightning and bacteria can change nitrogen into a different form.

2. _____ Denitrifying bacteria and nitrogen-fixing bacteria perform the same job.

3. _____ Nitrogen is found in both the ground and the air.

4. _____ Earth's atmosphere is made almost completely of oxygen.

5. _____ Most plants and animals can use the free nitrogen found in the atmosphere.

6. _____ Fertilizers that contain nitrates can upset the balance of nitrogen in nature.

Write your answers on the lines below.

7. What is the role of nitrogen-fixing bacteria?

   _____

8. What are two sources of free nitrogen in the soil?

   _____

9. Explain why too many nitrates in a body of water can be a problem.

   _____

10. How do nitrates used in fertilizers make their way into bodies of water, like lakes and streams?

   _____

11. What is a source of nitrogen for carnivores, or meat-eating animals?

   _____

Unifying Concepts and Processes

The nitrogen cycle is just one of many natural cycles that take place on Earth. Give an example of another cycle. Explain one thing that it has in common with the nitrogen cycle.

_____

_____

_____

Follow That Trail!

pheromones: chemicals that animals release to affect the behavior of other animals

emit: to give off or send out

gland: a cell, tissue, or organ in the body that secretes substances, such as saliva or sweat

A male silkworm moth can follow a pheromone trail nearly 30 miles to mate with a female silkworm moth.

One way human beings control pests is by releasing a pheromone near a crop that needs protection. The male insect becomes confused because the entire area seems to be filled with females, but it cannot find any of them. This prevents the insect from mating and reproducing.

The queen is the only insect that reproduces in a colony of ants or bees. By releasing a pheromone, she keeps the other females from being able to reproduce. This ensures that she keeps her status as queen.

Can insects and other animals use chemicals to communicate?

Odors can have a powerful effect. The smell of cookies baking or hamburgers on the grill can make your stomach rumble. The smell of something rotting can make you feel ill and cause you to move away from it.

Insects and other animals rely on something similar to odor to communicate with one another. **Pheromones** are chemicals that animals release to affect the behavior of other animals, usually of the same species. Pheromones are often carried through the air, like odors are, but they can also be found on the ground or other surfaces. The most common use of pheromones in insects is to attract a mate. For example, a female moth releases a pheromone when it is searching for a partner. When the male moth recognizes the odor, it follows the scent to the female.

Some pest-control companies take advantage of this behavior. They create products that contain pheromones that are similar to those released by common pests, such as Japanese beetles and gypsy moths. When beetles and moths fly to the source of the fake pheromone, they are trapped or killed.

Mating isn't the only use of pheromones, however. Social insects—insects that live in groups, like bees and ants—also use pheromones to coordinate life in their communities. Ants actually have several different pheromones that they can release, depending on the situation. When they discover a source of food, they create a trail of pheromones so that others in their colony can find it easily. They **emit** a different pheromone to warn of danger or an attack. When bees feel threatened, they can call for back-up from other bees in the hive by releasing an alarm pheromone.

Human beings aren't the only creatures that have found a way to imitate pheromones and use them for different purposes. Some insects produce pheromones similar to other species. They use these pheromones to lure unsuspecting followers. For example, one type of spider makes a pheromone that is similar to one produced by a female moth. This lures the male moth to the spider, where it is captured and eaten.

Mammals, like dogs, also use pheromones. Instead of emitting them from a **gland** as some other species do, their pheromones are released in urine. Have you ever heard someone say that a dog is "marking its spot"? It's actually leaving pheromones to let other dogs know where the boundaries of its territory are.

Circle the letter of the best answer to each question below.

1. Which of the following is an example of an animal using pheromones?

   a. A beetle laying its eggs under a log

   b. A worker bee providing food for the other bees in the hive

   c. An ant leaving a trail to a piece of bread

   d. Both a and c

2. A dog uses pheromones to

   a. warn other dogs of danger.

   b. lead other dogs to sources of food.

   c. defend its young.

   d. mark its territory.

Write your answers on the lines below.

3. What role do pheromones play in the mating of some insects?

   _____

4. Pheromones are usually a form of communication between animals of the same species. Give an example of a situation in which an animal of one species would use pheromones to communicate with an animal of a different species.

   _____

   _____

5. Why do you think social insects are among the creatures that use pheromones?

   _____

6. Explain why using pheromones to control populations of pests can be more Earth-friendly than other means.

   _____

7. What are two messages an animal or insect could send using pheromones?

   _____

   _____

Group Living

colony: a group of individuals of the same species that live together and depend on one another

castes: groups of organisms that have a specialized function within a society

cellulose: a material that makes up the cell walls of plants

Some species of termites build hills or mounds that can reach 25 to 30 feet in height. The mounds are built of soil, clay, saliva, chewed-up wood, and waste, which bake into a hard mass under the hot sun.

Lizards, birds, snakes, and other insects sometimes make their homes in termite nests. Some types of beetles produce a substance that termites eat. In exchange for the food, the beetles are allowed to live with the termites, using the nest as shelter and feeding on the termites' waste or eggs.

Why do termites live in groups called colonies?

Many people think that termites are a type of ant. They look similar to ants, and they share many habits. However, termites are actually more closely related to wood-eating cockroaches than they are to ants. There are more than 2,700 known species of termites, many of which live in rain forests and other tropical areas. In North America, they are often considered pests because some types destroy wooden structures.

Termites are social insects that live in colonies of 100 to several million. Each termite has a role in the community. By playing its role, the termite insures its own survival and the survival of the **colony**.

There are **castes**, or specialized groups, of termites in each colony—the reproductives, the soldiers, and the workers. The reproductives grow wings and leave the nests where they were born. Once they have flown to a different site, they shed their wings and mate. Each colony has only one set of royalty, and their main purpose is to produce eggs. In some tropical species, the king and queen can live for as long as 70 years. During this time, the queen can produce approximately 30,000 eggs a day.

The job of the workers is to build and take care of the nest, to care for the eggs and young, and to feed and groom the other termites. There are many jobs to be done, and the work is never-ending. For this reason, there are more workers than there are termites of other castes.

Soldiers have the important job of protecting the colony. They have strong jaws, called *mandibles*, and some species also have teeth. The combination can be deadly to attackers, like ants, that venture too close to the nest. In some species of termites, the soldiers are able to release a sticky, poisonous substance that disables their enemies.

Termites feed on **cellulose**, which is mostly found in wood, grass, and leaves. Cellulose is hard to digest, and termites wouldn't get any nutrition without the help of tiny creatures that live inside them. Protozoa are single-celled organisms that live in a termite's gut. They produce enzymes that break the cellulose down into usable parts for the termite.

Human beings tend to dislike termites because of their destructive habits. With a history spanning more than a hundred million years, though, it looks like the wood-loving creatures are here to stay.

Write **true** or **false** next to each statement below.

1. _____ Some types of termites have a relationship with beetles in which both the termite and the beetle benefit.

2. _____ The teeth of soldier termites are called mandibles.

3. _____ Termite queens produce only one batch of eggs before they die.

4. _____ Termite workers are in charge of building and repairing the nest.

5. _____ In a colony, there are more reproductives than workers or soldiers.

6. _____ Many species of termites live in damp, warm areas of the world.

Write your answers on the lines below.

7. In your own words, explain what a caste is.

   _____

8. Why do you think termites live in a colony instead of individually?

   _____

   _____

9. List one job that each termite below performs.

   reproductive: _____   worker: _____

   soldier: _____

10. Why do human beings find termites destructive?

   _____

11. Why do termites need to rely on the protozoa that live inside them?

   _____

Unifying Concepts and Processes

What method of investigation do you think scientists use to study the behavior of termites and learn about their systems of organization? Do you think that more than one method can be used? Explain.

   _____

adaptations: adjustments to conditions in the environment

deciduous: shedding leaves during cold or dry periods of weather

dispersed: spread out

Baobab trees have a longer life span than almost any other tree, but it's hard to tell their exact age. The growth rings in the trunks aren't a reliable measure as they are in most trees, since the baobabs' fibers are so spongy. Carbon dating, the process scientists use to date fossils, has shown that baobabs can live to be 2,000 to 3,000 years old.

Human beings have found uses for nearly every part of the baobab. The fruit can be made into a drink or a porridge. The leaves are eaten fresh or dried. The strong, fire-resistant fiber from the bark is made into rope and cloth. Parts of the tree can even be used to treat various illnesses.

What is a baobab tree? Why does it have such an unusual trunk?

With its wide, lumpy trunk, oddly-shaped fruit, and spindly bare branches, the baobab tree looks like something a cartoonist might have created. Each of its strange features serves a purpose, though, and helps the tree survive in its environment.

There are eight species of the Adansonia, or baobab, tree. Six of them can be found on the large island Madagascar, off the coast of Africa. The other two species are found in Africa and Australia.

Because they live in dry regions of the world, baobab trees have several important **adaptations**. The trunks are very wide, measuring as much as 30 feet across. The largest trunks are nearly 100 feet wide. These bulb-like trunks can store thousands of gallons of water. The reserves come in handy during the long, dry season when there is little rainfall. In Africa, elephants pierce the trunks with their tusks to get to the water. Even human beings tap the trees for their water supply.

The unusual trunks have other uses in the ecosystem, too. Hollowed out areas provide shelter for animals as diverse as squirrels, snakes, and scorpions. Cavities in the tree are an ideal place for birds, such as hornbills, parrots, and owls, to nest. Some of the larger trees have even been used as temporary shelters for human beings.

Baobab trees are **deciduous**, which means that they lose their leaves. In cool climates, deciduous trees shed their leaves during the cold winter months. In tropical climates, trees like the baobab lose their leaves during the dry season so that they can conserve energy. This means that for about nine months of the year, the tree appears to be lifeless because of its bare branches.

Baobabs bloom only once a year. The white flowers open at dusk and stay open for a single night. This is the tree's only chance to be pollinated, so the flowers have a strong odor, which attracts bats and insects. The fertilized flowers produce a fruit that is commonly known as *monkey bread*. When the fruit falls to the ground, animals eat it. The hard seeds are **dispersed** in the animals' waste. Before long, the next generation of these ancient and unusual trees has taken root.

Circle the letter of the best answer to each question below.

1. The baobab tree is well suited to life in a

   a. hot, dry climate.

   b. cool, dry climate.

   c. hot, wet climate.

   d. cool, wet climate.

2. It's difficult to tell exactly how old a baobab tree is because

   a. there are very few baobab trees still alive today.

   b. the fibers are spongy, which means that the growth rings don't accurately measure age.

   c. no one wants to cut down the trees to count their growth rings.

   d. baobab trees are only located in remote areas of the world.

Write your answers on the lines below.

3. Why do baobab trees have such enormous trunks?

   _____

4. What are three ways in which human beings use the baobab tree?

   _____

5. How are baobab trees an important part of their ecosystem? Give three examples.

   _____

   _____

6. What role do animals play in the baobab's reproduction?

   _____

7. Explain why the baobab's flowers are white and strongly scented.

   _____

8. Why do deciduous trees shed their leaves?

   _____

ecosystem: an environment, the plants and animals that live in it, and the way these parts interact with one another

habitat: the natural environment of a plant or animal

endangered: in danger, especially meaning animals in danger of extinction

manatees: large mammals with paddle-like arms and rounded tails that live in the water

The Everglades are the only place in the world where both alligators and crocodiles can be found.

The largest alligator ever spotted in Florida measured 17 feet 5 inches long.

Baby alligators stay near their mothers for up to two years, often riding on their mothers' heads or backs. This is because many animals will try to eat the babies— often the same animals that an adult alligator will eat.

How are changes in the Everglades affecting the animal community?

The Florida Everglades cover about 5,000 square miles of southern Florida. It's a unique **ecosystem** of water, tropical plants, and rare animals. Several different kinds of environments are found in the Everglades, such as wild forests, swamplands, and tidal pools. However, most of the Everglades consists of an extremely wide, shallow river that flows slowly from Lake Okeechobee all the way to Florida's south and west coasts. This river is only three feet deep in most places, and at one time, it was nearly 40 miles wide. It's nicknamed "the River of Grass" because grasses up to 10 feet high grow throughout the waterway. A network of open water trails crisscrosses the grassy river.

This area is the **habitat** for many creatures, including fish, frogs, turtles, snakes, storks, pelicans, bald eagles, deer, bobcats, butterflies, and, of course, mosquitoes. In the dry winter, the marsh changes into grassland dotted with pools of trapped fish. Alligators make "gator holes" in the pools by digging out plants with their snouts and feet. Then, they can feed on birds, raccoons, and deer that come to feed on the fish.

The marsh has changed a lot in the last hundred years. Cities on the coast grew much bigger, and highways were built across the Everglades. In 1900, new canals started carrying some of the water to these cities. A large part of the wetland was drained so the land could be farmed. Pesticides from the farms and mercury from fossil fuels have polluted the water.

The plants and animals in an ecosystem are deeply connected to the land. Because of the shrinking habitats, pollution, and hunting, many animals in the Everglades are now **endangered**. Biologists estimate that less than 50 Florida panthers still roam the area. The population of crocodiles is only a few hundred. Motorboats are another threat. Their blades slice open the backs of West Indian **manatees** that float just below the water's surface.

A federal law made hunting endangered animals illegal in 1969, and today, people are working hard to restore the land, too. Everglades National Park was expanded in 1989 to preserve almost 30 percent of the land. More laws passed recently have begun to reduce pollution and to change farmland back into natural habitat. Alligators, which were once endangered, are now a common sight. With a little more effort from human beings, more endangered species are sure to become plentiful once again.

NAME _____

Circle the letter of the best answer to each question below.

1. Which of the following environments can be found in the Florida Everglades?

   a. swamp

   b. river

   c. marshland

   d. All of the above

2. Almost all the damage done to the Florida Everglades ecosystem was caused by

   a. hurricanes.

   b. alligators and crocodiles.

   c. human beings.

   d. flooding.

Write your answers on the lines below.

3. Name two sources for the pollution that has ended up in the Everglades.

   _____   _____

4. Almost half of the original Everglades has been drained. What was the main reason for this?

   _____

5. A major interstate highway runs across the Everglades. In the late 1980s, this freeway was redesigned so that it had many more bridges, allowing water to flow more freely underneath it. How do you think this benefited wildlife in the Everglades?

   _____

   _____

6. Florida is one of the fastest growing states in America. What do you think would happen to the Everglades if laws weren't passed to protect it? What effect would this have on human beings?

   _____

   _____

   _____

Review

Circle the letter of the best answer to each question below.

1. A gene is

   a. a blueprint for DNA.

   b. a sequence of genomes.

   c. a small chromosome.

   d. a specific sequence of chemicals in DNA.

2. Which of the following organisms do not reproduce using spores?

   a. maple trees

   b. ferns

   c. moss

   d. fungi

3. The amount of nitrogen in the soil, water, and air have become unbalanced because

   a. fish produce too many nitrates.

   b. human beings have destroyed too many plants.

   c. human beings use too many fertilizers.

   d. human beings grow crops that don't use very many nitrates.

4. Why have some of the Everglades animals become endangered?

   a. Their habitats have become smaller.

   b. Human beings are no longer protecting them.

   c. Pollution has increased.

   d. Both a and c

Write your answers on the lines below.

5. What is one difference between plant and animal cells?

   _____

6. Why do you think cells are called *the building blocks of life*?

   _____

7. What is the purpose of the Galápagos finches' specialized beaks?

   _____

8. The Human Genome Project began in 1990. The scientists completed mapping the human genome in 2003. Why do you think it took so long?

_____

9. Why do plants need nitrogen-fixing bacteria?

_____

10. What are two messages an insect might communicate by using pheromones?

_____   _____

11. Why is the caste system in a termite colony important?

_____

12. What characteristics of the baobab tree allow it to live in a dry environment?

_____

13. What are two uses human beings have found for the baobab tree?

_____

14. What characteristics make the Florida Everglades such a unique ecosystem?

_____

Write **true** or **false** next to each statement below.

15. _____ The nucleus of a cell controls what happens inside the cell.

16. _____ The theory of natural selection explains why a finch's beak size or shape might change over time.

17. _____ No two human beings can share the same DNA.

18. _____ Each generation of a fern looks the same.

19. _____ Pheromones are produced only by insects.

20. _____ Termites are types of ants that build tall mounds and eat cellulose.

21. _____ A tree that loses its leaves every autumn is a deciduous tree.

22. _____ The Everglades is the only place on Earth where both alligators and crocodiles are found.

Mid-Test

Circle the letter of the best answer to each question below.

1. An ice cube melts

   a. when heat brings energy to its molecules and causes them to move more rapidly.

   b. because energy is leaving its molecules and moving into the matter around it.

   c. because gases in the air mix with the ice and turn it into a liquid.

   d. when the solid molecules are broken apart by thermodynamics.

2. A cell's nucleus

   a. contains DNA.

   b. is one of several organelles found inside the cell.

   c. is where cell division begins.

   d. All of the above

Write your answers on the lines below.

3. Name two safety precautions you should take when working in the lab.

   _____

4. Why are experiments such important tools for scientists?

   _____

5. How did animals become trapped in the La Brea Tar Pits?

   _____

6. Why did scientists reject Wegener's theory of continental drift at first?

   _____

7. What did the three different groups receive in Salk's polio vaccine study?

   _____

8. Explain the difference between an ion and an isotope.

   _____

9. Does a car moving 10 miles per hour have the same inertia as a baseball moving 10 miles per hour? What does your answer tell you about inertia?

   _____

10. How does friction create static electricity?

_____

11. When a bird flaps its wings, they create _____ to get the bird into the air and

_____ to move the bird forward.

12. Use potential and kinetic energy to describe the swing of a pendulum.

_____

13. Acids have a pH _____ than seven, and bases have a pH _____
than seven.

14. What is natural selection?

_____

15. What function do spores perform for organisms like fungi and molds?

_____

16. What are pheromones?

_____

17. What role do animals play in the nitrogen cycle?

_____

18. How do animals in the baobab's ecosystem make use of the baobab tree?

_____

On the line, write the letter of the definition in column two that matches the word in column one.

19. _____ excavating   **a.** ready to break apart, change, or react

20. _____ conductors   **b.** a tiny packet of electromagnetic radiation or energy

21. _____ unstable   **c.** digging up; unearthing

22. _____ chromosome   **d.** two or more elements that have combined together chemically

23. _____ photon   **e.** substances that allow electricity to easily pass through them

24. _____ adoption   **f.** adjustments to conditions in the environment

25. _____ compound   **g.** molecules of DNA in the nucleus

Lesson 4.1   The Restless Continents

ridge: a line of hills or mountains

magma: rock from deep inside Earth that has turned to liquid because of high temperatures and pressure

boundaries: dividing lines or borders between two areas

lithosphere: the layer of Earth's structure that is broken into tectonic plates; it sits on a layer of molten, or melted, rock that allows the plates to move

mantle: the largest of the three major layers that make up Earth's structure; the other two layers are the crust and the core

Most volcanoes are located where plates meet because magma has the best chance of reaching Earth's surface through these cracks in the crust.

Tectonic plates move very slowly—only a few centimeters per year. Over a period of 130 million years, though, the Atlantic Ocean was formed as the Americas slowly moved away from Europe and Africa.

How were Wegener's ideas about continental drift proven correct?

When Alfred Wegener introduced his idea of continental drift in 1915, he was met with ridicule. Scientists didn't believe something as massive as a continent could move around Earth's surface. Even if continents could move, they asked, how did it happen? Wegener admitted he didn't have the answer.

Then, in the 1950s, scientists used new technologies to map the ocean floor. They soon discovered a gigantic, undersea mountain range in the Atlantic Ocean. It stretched almost the entire length from the North to the South Poles. They named it the *Mid-Atlantic Ridge*.

Scientists learned that this **ridge** formed—and was still growing—because **magma** rose through a crack in Earth's surface and then cooled. As the ridge grew wider, it pushed Earth's crust away in opposite directions—a process called *seafloor spreading*. Scientists had just discovered one of the many **boundaries** between Earth's plates. By the 1960s, more of these boundaries had been discovered, and the theory of plate tectonics was born.

Earth's **lithosphere**—a layer that includes the crust and the upper part of the **mantle**—is broken into several large sections, called *plates*. Because Earth's surface isn't solid, magma rises to the surface in the cracks between plates. Wherever the rising magma causes seafloor spreading, the plates are pushed away from each other. Wegener didn't live to see it, but this process answered the question of how Earth's continents moved.

Wegener's theory of continental drift wasn't exactly right, though. The continents move, but a continent is just one part of a much larger plate—the part that rises above sea level.

Earth's plates are packed tightly together. Whenever two plates are pushed away from each other, their edges press against the edges of other plates. In some places, plates push directly against each other, and the land buckles and rises at the edges to form mountains. In other places, the edge of one plate is driven underneath the other plate. This is called *subduction*.

Wherever plates meet, there's a good chance for geological activity. This is because plates don't slide smoothly past each other. Instead, friction causes pressure to build as the plates try to move. After enough pressure has been created, the plates will break free and move in one sudden motion. This powerful movement is felt on Earth's surface as an earthquake.

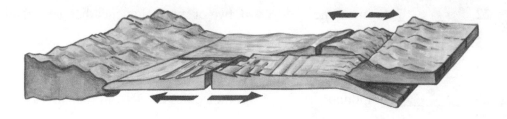

Circle the letter of the best answer to each question below.

1. What is magma?

   a. rocks found in Earth's crust

   b. liquid rock formed deep below Earth's surface

   c. the largest type of tectonic plate

   d. a mountain range found deep under the ocean

2. Seafloor spreading causes the surrounding plates to

   a. move away from each other.

   b. crash into each other.

   c. slide along next to each other.

   d. break up into smaller plates.

Write your answers on the lines below.

3. Explain why the discovery of how the Mid-Atlantic Ridge formed was important to developing the theory of plate tectonics.

   _____

   _____

4. Wegener thought continents drifted through the oceans. Why is this idea incorrect?

   _____

5. What part of Wegener's theory of continental drift was correct?

   _____

Unifying Concepts and Processes

Review the definitions of potential and kinetic energy from the previous chapter. Explain the role each type of energy plays in the cause and occurrence of earthquakes.

_____

_____

_____

Carving Out the Grand Canyon

erosion: the movement of rock and soil by natural means, such as wind and rain

sediments: soil or other matter that has settled at the bottom of a liquid

plateau: a high flat land; tableland; also called a *mesa* in Spanish

strata: layers

marine: of the sea

iron oxide: iron that has reacted chemically with oxygen, better known as *rust*

Arizona is very dry, and much of the land there is desert, so how does erosion occur? The rain that does fall comes in big, powerful storms that dump a lot of water onto the land at once. Desert plants have short roots that help them absorb this water as it floods the desert's surface, but these shallow roots don't hold the soil in place. The rushing water carries some of the desert away with it.

How did a river form one of the biggest canyons in the world?

The Grand Canyon is one of America's most famous landmarks. This enormous canyon stretches for 277 miles through northwest Arizona and is nearly a mile deep in most parts. The colorful layers of rock that line the canyon walls were exposed by the Colorado River as it carved out the canyon over a period of millions of years. This mighty river still flows through the bottom of the canyon today.

About 60 million years ago, movement of Earth's tectonic plates formed the Rocky Mountains rising to the north of the Grand Canyon. Every spring since then, the mountain snows melt, and water runs downhill in streams and rivers. About six million years ago, **erosion** formed the Colorado River. The river carried its **sediments** downstream, and they wore away at the landscape and slowly dug out the canyon.

As the river began to carve its path, the land around it was also rising because of movement in Earth's crust. Between five and 10 million years ago, the land west of the Rocky Mountains formed a high, flat area called a **plateau**. This rising land made the river deeper. It also made the Northern Rim of the Grand Canyon more than one thousand feet higher than the Southern Rim.

The Northern Rim is not only higher, but also colder than the Southern Rim. The two sides have very different environments—forests grow to the north, but the south is a desert.

All the water from the north side drains into the canyon. Some flows into cracks in the rocks. In winter, this water freezes and expands, causing rocks to break off and fall into the canyon—another form of erosion.

Over time, the growing canyon exposed about 20 **strata**, or layers, of different colored rock. Each layer was formed by sediment that turned into rock hundreds of millions of years ago. Most of it is **marine** sediment, which tells geologists that the land was once under water. Some of the layers even contain fossils of sea creatures, including sharks and squid.

The red layers in the canyon contain **iron oxide**, and the bottom layer is black rock from about two billion years ago. Scientists think this rock may have once been a mountain range that was even bigger than the Rockies. As old as the Colorado River is, it's quite young compared to the black rocks at the canyon's bottom.

Circle the letter of the best answer to each question below.

1. Over a period of millions of years, erosion caused by the _____ carved out the Grand Canyon.

   a. Arizona River

   b. Colorado River

   c. Grand River

   d. Rocky Mountains

2. Much of the water that flows through the canyon starts as

   a. sediment.

   b. erosion.

   c. snow.

   d. iron oxide.

3. What did geologists conclude based on the fossils and sediments found in the canyon's different layers of rock?

   a. The fossils were carried there by the Colorado River.

   b. The fossils became buried in sediment when the Rocky Mountains formed.

   c. The Northern Rim is much older than the Southern Rim.

   d. The area where the Grand Canyon formed used to be undersea.

Write your answers on the lines below.

4. What role did plate tectonics play in forming the Grand Canyon?

   _____

5. Do you think the Grand Canyon is still growing? Explain your answer.

   _____

   _____

Unifying Concepts and Processes

If the layer of black rocks at the bottom of the Grand Canyon is two billion years old, what does this tell you about how old Earth is?

_____

Set in Stone

lagoons: shallow bodies of water connected to larger bodies of water

salinity: amount or level of saltiness

scavengers: organisms that feed on dead plant and animal materials

For years, the limestone at Solnhofen was dug up from large pits called *quarries*. The limestone was used to build walls, roofs, floors, and roads. Quarry workers discovered many fossils and were often allowed to keep them until interest in the fossils grew and their value became known.

The archaeopteryx was a cross between a bird and a dinosaur. It had feathers and wings, but its skeleton and teeth resembled those of dinosaurs. It was about the size of a crow but had a long, bony tail. Scientists believe it was cold-blooded, unlike modern birds. Many people consider it a "missing link" because it appears to bridge the gap between reptiles and birds.

Does the quality of fossils vary depending on where they are found?

One hundred and fifty-five million years ago, during the Jurassic period, the world was a very different place. Earth's single landmass, Pangaea, had begun to separate into two continents. Dinosaurs roamed the planet, and the first birds appeared. Plant and animal life were flourishing.

A warm sea covered much of what is modern Germany. The waters were shallow and supported coral reefs that separated the water into **lagoons**. Water didn't flow quickly between these lagoons and the ocean, so the **salinity**, or level of salt, in the lagoons was very high. With low levels of oxygen and high levels of salt, few organisms could survive in the water.

Occasionally, animals would fall into the lagoons. The bodies of other animals washed into the water from the oceans or from nearby islands. In the ocean or in a large lake, the remains of the animals might have been eaten by **scavengers** or broken down by strong currents. Even scavengers couldn't survive in the lagoon water, so the remains lay undisturbed in the soft mud.

The result was that even delicate animals could be preserved in great detail. In most fossils, only the hard parts of an animal, like its bones and teeth, are preserved. In the limestone found in Solnhofen, Germany—an area where the lagoons were once located—amazing impressions have been found. Paleontologists have located fossils of soft-bodied jellyfish and delicate dragonflies. In all, more than 750 different species of plants and animals have been identified in the Solnhofen limestone.

The most important discovery was the fossil of an archaeopteryx. Experts believe that the archaeopteryx was the first bird and is a link between dinosaurs and modern birds. Feathers aren't usually preserved in fossils because they are delicate and decompose quickly. In a specimen found in Solnhofen, though, the archaeopteryx's feathers can be seen. Only ten archaeopteryx fossils have ever been found, all of them in Solnhofen limestone.

Learning about life in prehistoric times is a little like putting together a puzzle. Each new piece that's found allows scientists to get a better idea of what the big picture looks like. The fossils discovered in Solnhofen, Germany, have filled in many pieces of the picture of life on Earth during the Jurassic period.

Circle the letter of the best answer to each question below.

1. Why couldn't living creatures survive in the Solnhofen lagoons?

   a. The salinity was too high.

   b. The water was too cold during much of the year.

   c. There wasn't enough oxygen in the water.

   d. Both a and c

2. Which of the following would be least likely to be fossilized outside of Solnhofen?

   a. a shark's tooth

   b. the jaw of a dinosaur

   c. a bird's leg bone

   d. the body of a jellyfish

Write **true** or **false** next to each statement below.

3. _____ Archaeopteryx fossils have been discovered all around the world.

4. _____ Coral reefs helped create the lagoons in Solnhofen.

5. _____ Only plant life existed during the Jurassic Period.

6. _____ As far as scientists know, Earth has always been divided into seven continents.

7. _____ Soft-tissue parts of animals are rarely preserved in fossils.

Write your answers on the lines below.

8. Why was the discovery of the archaeopteryx so important?

   _____

9. What is unusual about the fossils found in Solnhofen limestone?

   _____

10. How were many of the early Solnhofen fossils discovered?

   _____

11. Would the Solnhofen fossil specimens have been as complete if scavengers were able to survive in the lagoons? Explain.

   _____

crust: the outermost of the three layers that make up Earth's structure; the mantle lies below the crust, and the core is at Earth's center

submarine: underwater

subduction: the process by which one plate will be pushed underneath the other plate when two opposing plates meet

oceanic trenches: deep areas in the ocean created by subduction

Not all islands are located where plates meet. For example, undersea volcanoes formed the Hawaiian Islands, but they aren't anywhere near the edge of a tectonic plate. These volcanoes are located over vents that feed magma to the surface with enough pressure to break through the plate. The magma still cools when it hits the water, though, and slowly builds a mountain.

Measured from its base on the ocean floor, the Hawaiian mountain Mauna Kea is taller than Mount Everest.

What does Earth look like deep below the oceans?

Earth's oceans are deep. On average, the ocean floor is more than two miles below sea level. Eight Empire State Buildings could be stacked on top of each other and still not break the surface. Of course, that depth is just an average. The ocean floor is anything but flat. It rises and falls just like all the land in Earth's **crust**.

The crust is much thinner under the oceans than it is on land, though. This means magma coming up from Earth's mantle doesn't have far to travel to reach the surface. Undersea mountain ranges, called *mid-ocean ridges*, are formed where magma steadily rises through the spaces between tectonic plates. When the magma emerges, it hits water and quickly cools, adding another layer to the ridge.

Sometimes, the peaks of these mountains rise above the ocean's surface to form islands. For example, the East Pacific Rise is the mid-ocean ridge running off the western coast of South America. Near Ecuador, the peaks are tall enough to poke up out of the waves, and the mountaintops form the Galápagos Islands.

Volcanoes are the most common way that magma reaches Earth's surface. As you might expect, they're usually located at plate boundaries because that's where magma can find its way through the crust. Almost three-quarters of the magma that reaches Earth's surface travels through **submarine** volcanoes. They usually don't explode like volcanoes on land, though. Deep below the ocean's surface, high pressure is created by the weight of all that water, so magma oozes out of the crust instead.

Earth's mid-ocean ridges form a continuous chain of undersea mountains and volcanoes wrapping around Earth. Imagine the seams on a baseball, and you'll get an idea of how they circle the planet. As the magma flows out, the ridges continue to grow, and they cause seafloor spreading. This process pushes Earth's plates around the planet and into each other.

When tectonic plates are driven into one another, one plate will slide underneath the other. This process, called **subduction**, creates deep **oceanic trenches** where the plates meet. These undersea valleys are the deepest spots in Earth's crust. The Marianas Trench, located south of Japan in the Pacific Ocean, is the deepest on Earth. The ocean floor there is more than six-and-a-half miles below the surface.

Circle the letter of the best answer to each question below.

1. In places where seafloor spreading is occurring, you would expect to see

   a. a mid-ocean ridge.

   b. an oceanic trench.

   c. volcanoes.

   d. Both a and c

2. Volcanoes are _____ found where two plates meet.

   a. never

   b. rarely

   c. often

   d. always

3. Earth's crust is _____ under the oceans than it is on land.

   a. thicker

   b. thinner

   c. more solid

   d. Both a and c

Write your answers on the lines below.

4. Explain why submarine volcanoes seldom erupt with an explosion.

   _____

5. Where are oceanic trenches located? Be specific.

   _____

   _____

6. Mauna Kea rises about 14,000 feet above sea level, but Mount Everest rises about 29,000 feet above sea level. Why does the author say that Mauna Kea could actually be considered the tallest mountain on Earth?

   _____

Layers of the Sky

What do scientists call the different layers in Earth's atmosphere?

Earth is surrounded by a mixture of gases called an *atmosphere*. It doesn't float away into space because gravity holds the gases in place. Nitrogen is by far the most common gas in Earth's atmosphere. It makes up almost 80 percent of the total mass. Oxygen is second, making up about 20 percent, and about one percent is a mixture of other gases.

Although these gases extend for hundreds of miles above Earth, nearly three-quarters of their total mass is packed into the lowest and thinnest layer, called the *troposphere*. The troposphere is by far the **densest** of Earth's atmospheric layers. Its highest point varies from about five miles at Earth's poles, to about 10 miles at the equator.

Nearly all of Earth's **water vapor** is found in the troposphere. The weather we experience each day is created when gases and water vapor mix and move around in this lowest layer. When warm air near Earth's surface rises to mix with cooler air high in the troposphere, it carries water vapor with it. When the vapor cools, it condenses to form rain droplets and clouds.

The stratosphere begins where the troposphere ends and extends to about 30 miles above Earth's surface. The stratosphere contains the **ozone** layer. Ozone is a special oxygen molecule that absorbs much of the sun's harmful **ultraviolet radiation** that would otherwise reach the surface. Without the ozone layer, life wouldn't be possible on Earth.

Air rising through the troposphere cools, but it becomes warm again in the stratosphere. Temperatures rise there because UV light is being absorbed by the ozone layer.

The mesosphere is next. In this layer, temperatures fall once again. Most meteors that enter Earth's atmosphere burn up in this layer, so the mesosphere is the home of shooting stars.

About 55 miles above Earth, the mesosphere turns into the thermosphere. This layer stretches more than 400 miles, making it much thicker than the first three layers. Solar radiation causes the temperature to soar.

The final layer before entering outer space is the exosphere. It stretches thousands of miles above Earth. Only light gases, like hydrogen, can be found there, making it the perfect place for human-made satellites to orbit the planet without creating too much friction and heat.

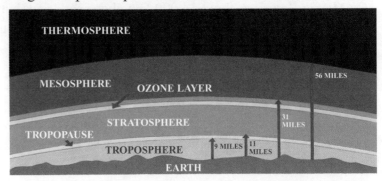

Circle the letter of the best answer to each question below.

1. Temperatures _____ as you travel higher through the troposphere.

   a. fall

   b. rise

   c. stay the same

   d. rise and fall

2. The ozone layer protects life on Earth from

   a. solar heat that would otherwise make the planet too warm for life.

   b. harmful ultraviolet radiation.

   c. a harmful oxygen molecule that contains three atoms.

   d. Both b and c

3. Shooting stars are meteors burning up in the

   a. thermosphere.

   b. exosphere.

   c. mesosphere.

   d. stratosphere.

Write your answers on the lines below.

4. Where is the mesopause located?

   _____

5. Jets usually travel through the stratosphere during their flights. Why do you think pilots choose to fly there instead of the lower troposphere?

   _____

What's Next?

Do other planets have atmospheres? Use a book or Web site that describes each of the planets in detail to find the answer. What kinds of gases are in the atmospheres of other planets? How are planets with atmospheres different from those without them? What would Earth be like without an atmosphere?

A Sky Full of Lights

aurora borealis: colorful lights that stream across the sky in the northern hemisphere; the result of solar wind colliding with Earth's gases

solar wind: a stream of charged particles that the sun constantly emits

magnetosphere: Earth's magnetic field

The electrical energy in the atmosphere during auroras can cause electrical disturbances on Earth. For example, it can cause power outages and interfere with satellites, TV transmissions, pagers, and cell phones.

Earth isn't the only planet to experience auroras. They occur on other planets that have an atmosphere and a magnetic field, such as Jupiter, Mars, Uranus, and Neptune. Auroras even occur on Io, one of Jupiter's moons. The Hubble Space Telescope has taken images of these auroras.

The aurora borealis can generally be seen in the northern parts of the United States, Canada, Russia, and Nordic countries, like Norway and Finland.

What causes the northern lights, and where can they be seen?

Imagine looking up on a clear night and seeing streaks of red, purple, and green shimmer and dance across the sky. It might seem hard to believe, but this colorful light show is put on by nature. The northern lights, also called the **aurora borealis**, can usually be seen during the spring and fall in northern parts of the world. The aurora can also be seen in the southern hemisphere. There, they are called the *aurora australis*. The southern and northern lights together are known as *aurora polaris*, which means "polar lights." Ever since human beings first caught sight of these colorful lights in the sky, they have been creating myths and legends to explain them. Today, a more scientific answer is available.

The sun plays an important role in the creation of the auroras. **Solar wind** is a stream of gas containing electrically charged particles. Although it moves extremely quickly—at speeds of more than a million miles per hour—it still takes two to three days for solar wind to travel the 93 million miles to Earth.

Earth's core is like a giant magnet. At either end of the planet are Earth's magnetic poles. They create a magnetic field called the **magnetosphere** that captures the solar particles as they approach Earth. Earth's atmosphere serves as a sort of shield or defense against solar wind. When the gases in the atmosphere come in contact with the charged solar particles, a collision occurs, which produces light. If this happened only once, the light wouldn't be visible. Because there are millions of collisions at once, though, enough light is generated to see the aurora from Earth.

No two auroras are ever alike. They can take a number of shapes, such as an arch, a band, curtains, and streamers. The colors that are produced have to do with what types of gas the particles strike and where in the atmosphere the collision occurs. Remember, Earth's atmosphere is made almost completely of nitrogen and oxygen. Green and red auroras tend to be the result of collisions with oxygen atoms. Blue and purple lights are usually created when the solar particles hit nitrogen atoms. Auroras can last from a few seconds to a few hours, depending on the conditions.

If you're ever lucky enough to see an aurora, try to capture a photograph of it. People often travel long distances with the hope that they'll get a chance to witness one of nature's most beautiful spectacles.

NAME _____

Circle the letter of the best answer to each question below.

1. In which of the following places would you be most likely to see the aurora borealis?

    a. Virginia

    b. New Mexico

    c. Maine

    d. Louisiana

2. What does a planet need to have in order for auroras to take place?

    a. a moon

    b. a magnetic field

    c. an atmosphere

    d. Both b and c

3. Which of the following statements is true?

    a. The color of an aurora depends on what type of gas the solar particles hit.

    b. Auroras can be seen only in the northern hemisphere.

    c. It takes solar wind nearly a week to reach Earth.

    d. Another name for aurora borealis is aurora australis.

Write your answers on the lines below.

4. What is solar wind?

_____

_____

5. What effect can auroras have on Earth?

_____

6. What happens when solar wind approaches Earth's atmosphere?

_____

7. Why do you think no two auroras are ever the same?

_____

Soaring Through Space

axis: an imaginary straight line running through Earth from pole to pole and around which Earth rotates

circumference: the distance around a circle or a sphere

plane: in mathematics, a flat, two-dimensional surface

ecliptic: the path taken by the sun and planets through Earth's sky

precession: the slow circling of the axis of a rotating body

Solar days are 24 hours, but a sidereal (sī dear ē əl) day is four minutes shorter. A sidereal day is based on the amount of time Earth needs to complete one rotation in relation to the stars, not the sun. Solar days are four minutes longer because Earth has to rotate a tiny bit farther in order for the same spot to be facing the sun again. This is because Earth moved along its orbit as it spun.

How quickly does Earth travel around the sun?

Earth is always in motion. Every day, it completes one rotation on its **axis**. You are always moving with Earth. Depending on where you live, it carries you along at different speeds.

Earth's spherical shape means that someone at the equator moves much more quickly than someone standing near the poles. Earth's **circumference** is about 25,000 miles at the equator. In 24 hours—the time it takes Earth to make one rotation—you travel that entire distance. The closer someone stands to the poles, though, the less distance they will travel in 24 hours, which means they are moving more slowly than someone at the equator.

Of course, Earth doesn't just spin in place. It also orbits the sun once every year. Earth zooms along at 67,000 miles per hour in order to make its 580-million-mile journey around the sun in 365 days.

Like the other planets' orbits, the path of Earth's orbit is shaped almost like a circle. All of the planets move around the sun on nearly the same **plane**, the plane of the **ecliptic**. It's like an imaginary flat disk surrounding the sun, similar to the rings of Saturn.

Earth's axis doesn't stand upright in relation to the sun. It tilts, or leans, about 23 degrees from being vertical. This tilt causes the seasons. When Earth is on one side of the sun, the tilt places the southern hemisphere closer to the sun's warmth. The bottom half of the planet experiences summer, while the top half goes through winter. When Earth reaches the other side of the sun, the tilt doesn't change, but the top half of the planet is now closer to the sun. The northern hemisphere gets its summer, while the southern hemisphere cools down.

Earth's spin isn't perfect. It wobbles just a bit, like a spinning top beginning to slow down. If you looked down at the North Pole from space, you would see—over a period of thousands of years—that the axis slowly moves clockwise in a circle. Right now, the axis points toward Polaris, or the North Star. During the next 26,000 years, the axis will trace a circle in the sky as it points to different spots before pointing at Polaris again. This wobble is called **precession**.

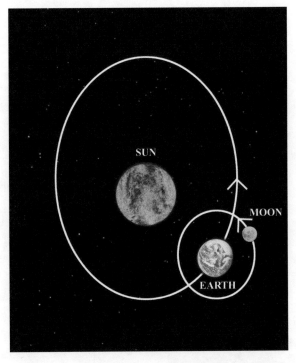

NAME _____

Circle the letter of the best answer to each question below.

1. Earth's axis is

    a. the imaginary line running through the poles.

    b. the path of Earth's orbit around the sun.

    c. the rotation Earth makes each day.

    d. the angle it tilts away from the sun.

2. Precession describes

    a. how Earth travels around the sun.

    b. Earth's wobble as it spins on its axis.

    c. the way Earth's axis tilts to create the seasons.

    d. how the planets orbit the sun.

3. Earth's circumference is greatest

    a. at the equator.

    b. at the South Pole.

    c. at the North Pole.

    d. Both b and c

4. All the planets in our solar system circle the sun in nearly the same

    a. orbit.

    b. plane.

    c. speed.

    d. rotation.

Write your answer on the lines below.

5. Explain how Earth's movement around the sun creates the seasons.

    _____

    _____

    _____

Shrinking Pluto

Hubble Space Telescope: launched in 1990, this telescope orbits Earth and provides the clearest, most detailed views of space available to human beings

methane: a chemical compound of hydrogen and carbon; CH_4

reflective: capable of reflecting light

Kuiper Belt: the area beyond Neptune in which Pluto, Charon, and about 800 other objects discovered so far orbit the sun

Some scientists believe that Charon shouldn't really be considered a moon of Pluto. The two objects actually orbit each other—the center of the orbit lies between them—so they should be considered a double planet, or binary system, instead.

Pluto is smaller than seven of the moons orbiting other planets, including Earth's moon.

New Horizons will have traveled more than three billion miles by the time it reaches Pluto.

Just how tiny is Pluto?

On January 19, 2006, NASA launched the *New Horizons* spacecraft. It roared away from Earth at 36,260 miles per hour—faster than any other spacecraft before it. This quick take-off was planned to give *New Horizons* a good start in its long journey to the far reaches of our solar system. In 2015, it will become the first spacecraft to fly near the dwarf planet Pluto. What will *New Horizons* find when it gets there?

Pluto's orbit is about 40 times farther from the sun than Earth's. Because this tiny, frozen rock is so far away, human beings have never had a good look at it. Even the **Hubble Space Telescope** can't take a decent photo of Pluto.

Astronomers didn't always think Pluto was so small. It was originally predicted to be the giant Planet X that was thought to be affecting Uranus and Neptune's orbits. Scientists soon realized that Pluto wasn't a giant planet, and by the 1950s, it was thought to be about the size of Earth. By the early 1970s, Pluto was assumed to be the size of Mars. Then, two discoveries in the mid-70s revealed just how small Pluto really is.

First, astronomers studying Pluto's brightness determined that the dwarf planet contained frozen **methane**, which is a highly **reflective** substance. Using this information, astronomers calculated Pluto's mass to be no bigger than one percent of Earth's.

Then, in 1978, astronomers discovered that the single dot of light they saw as Pluto was, in fact, both Pluto and its nearby moon, Charon. Charon is more than half Pluto's size, making it the largest moon in the solar system compared to the object it orbits. All the calculations about Pluto's size had been including Charon, too. Today, we know that Pluto is only about one quarter of one percent of Earth's mass.

Although no details of Pluto's surface will be seen until *New Horizons* gets there, astronomers have used devices here on Earth to make discoveries about its composition. For example, the light waves that Pluto reflects show that its surface is nearly 98 percent frozen nitrogen.

Once *New Horizons* gets a look at Pluto, its journey will continue through the **Kuiper Belt** and beyond. The spacecraft's devices will be searching for any other large objects orbiting in these distant areas. So far, scientists know that at least one object out there—the dwarf planet Eris—is larger than Pluto. What else will *New Horizons* discover?

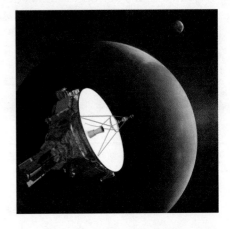

Circle the letter of the best answer to each question below.

1. Pluto's mass is

    a. about equal to the mass of Mars.

    b. about half the mass of its moon, Charon.

    c. less than one percent of Earth's mass.

    d. unknown.

2. Which of the following statements is not true?

    a. Pluto is the largest object orbiting beyond Neptune.

    b. Charon is more than half the size of Pluto.

    c. Eris is the largest of the dwarf planets.

    d. Pluto is found in the Kuiper Belt.

3. The Hubble Space Telescope can't get a good photograph of Pluto's surface because

    a. Charon's orbit blocks the view.

    b. Hubble is orbiting on the opposite side of Earth from Pluto.

    c. Pluto is too far away.

    d. space dust in the asteroid belt makes it too difficult to see.

Write your answer on the line below.

4. Why do some scientists think that Charon isn't a moon of Pluto?

_____

Unifying Concepts and Processes

Nitrogen is by far the most common element found in Earth's atmosphere. It's even more common on Pluto's surface. How does the nitrogen found in Earth's atmosphere differ from the nitrogen on Pluto's surface? What do you think causes this difference?

_____

_____

_____

galaxies: huge groups of billions of stars and other matter found throughout the universe

cosmologists: astronomers who study the beginning and structure of the universe, as well as the relationship between space and time

controversial: relating to or causing discussions about a subject or idea that people strongly disagree about

American astronomer Vesto Slipher was the first to notice that the galaxies were all speeding away from each other. At the time of his discovery, he was the director of the Lowell Observatory in Arizona and had hired Clyde Tombaugh, the man who discovered Pluto.

Albert Einstein's general theory of relativity, which combines all known ideas about space, time, and gravity, shows that the expanding universe can be traced backward to a single point of matter.

Do we know all there is to know about the universe?

Human beings have studied the skies for thousands of years and learned a great deal about the universe. Still, some great mysteries are yet to be solved. Here are just a few examples:

- In 1912, careful observations of the **galaxies** showed that they are all moving away from each other—the universe is expanding in all directions. It took several years and the work of many astronomers, but this discovery eventually led to the Big Bang Theory. This theory— widely accepted by **cosmologists** today—describes how the universe began as a single point of extraordinarily dense matter. No one knows why, but this matter suddenly exploded with great force and expanded almost instantly to the immense size of our universe today. Then, over billions of years, the pieces of matter combined to form stars, planets, and everything else in the universe. These pieces of matter are still forming today. This idea is **controversial**, but discoveries made since the Big Bang Theory was first proposed continue to support it. In the 1990s, research showed that the universe is not only expanding, but it's actually expanding at an increasing speed. What will happen as the universe and everything in it continues to spread out?

- Soon after galaxies were proven to exist, astronomers realized that they moved through space much more quickly than they should. By measuring a galaxy's mass, and then considering how gravity from other galaxies would affect it, astronomers made a prediction about its speed. When they actually measured the speeds, though, it was as if the galaxies had much greater masses than their stars would have provided. Astronomers concluded that the universe must contain huge amounts of "dark matter" that we can't detect, which would give the galaxies the mass they need. But what is dark matter, and will we ever be able to see it?

- In November of 2008, NASA plans to launch the Kepler Mission. It will be a space-based observatory searching for planets outside our solar system. Scientists know that a planet similar to Earth will have a greater chance of containing life. Evidence of water and carbon will be searched for because they are the basis of all life on Earth. Billions of galaxies, each one filled with billions of stars, leads many scientists to think that life exists somewhere else in space. When will we find the evidence?

Circle the letter of the best answer to each question below.

1. The Big Bang Theory states that

    a. the universe will end with a giant explosion.

    b. dark matter was created when a supernova exploded.

    c. the universe began as a single particle of matter.

    d. galaxies contain billions of stars.

2. Scientists know that

    a. galaxies are much heavier than they appear.

    b. the universe is expanding more quickly as time passes.

    c. water and carbon are found in all life forms on Earth.

    d. All of the above

Write your answers on the lines below.

3. What tells scientists that dark matter exists, even though it can't be seen?

    _____

    _____

4. So far, astronomers have identified 236 planets outside of our solar system. According to the selection, what evidence do scientists look for to determine whether or not a planet might have life?

    _____

5. Do you think human beings will ever find life in another part of the universe? Explain your answer.

    _____

    _____

What's Next?

The subjects mentioned in this selection are just three examples of many questions still facing cosmologists. Find out what is known and unknown about other cosmic mysteries, such as black holes, dark energy, and the shape of the universe.

Circle the letter of the best answer to each question below.

1. Why was the discovery of the archaeopteryx so important?

   a. It was the only dinosaur that lived in the Solnhofen lagoons.

   b. It provided evidence that dinosaurs could fly.

   c. Scientists thought it had become extinct much earlier in history.

   d. It provided scientists with a link between dinosaurs and birds.

2. What does a planet need in order to have auroras?

   a. nitrogen and oxygen

   b. an atmosphere and a magnetosphere

   c. an ozone layer and solar energy

   d. a lithosphere and subduction

3. What is the Kuiper Belt?

   a. The layer in Earth's structure that lies between the mantle and the core

   b. The part of Earth's atmosphere that contains the ozone layer

   c. An area of the solar system beyond Neptune that contains Pluto

   d. The area in the ocean where seafloor spreading occurs

4. In their search for life someplace other than Earth, scientists look for evidence of

   _____ because they are the basis of all life on Earth.

   a. oxygen and carbon dioxide

   b. carbon and water

   c. an atmosphere and weather

   d. trees and oceans

Write your answers on the lines below.

5. What causes Earth's plates to move?

   _____

6. What are two geological events that often occur where tectonic plates meet?

   _____   _____

7. What happens when an undersea mountain breaks through the ocean's surface?

_____

8. What did fossils found in the Grand Canyon's layers tell scientists about the region?

_____

9. Why are the fossils found in Solnhofen, Germany, unique?

_____

10. How does the ozone layer protect life on Earth?

_____

11. What is the most common element in Earth's atmosphere? _____

12. Explain the difference between the aurora borealis and the aurora australis.

_____

13. What effect does Earth's tilt have on the weather?

_____

14. What makes Pluto's moon, Charon, different from the moons that orbit other planets?

_____

15. Briefly describe the Big Bang Theory.

_____

Use the words in the box to complete the sentences below.

cosmology	precession	mantle	subduction	sediments

16. Earth's lithosphere contains the upper part of the _____ and the crust.

17. Erosion, caused by _____ moving down the Colorado River, created the Grand Canyon.

18. _____ occurs when the edge of one tectonic plate is driven underneath another plate.

19. Earth wobbles as it spins, which is a process called _____.

20. _____ is the study of the origins, events, and objects in the universe.

Lesson 5.1   The Beginning of Human Civilization

nomads: people without a permanent home who travel from place to place

foraged: searched for food

edible: safe to eat

Neolithic Age: the last part of the Stone Age; it began with the rise of farming and ended when human beings began using metal tools

Mesopotamia: an ancient culture located in the area that is Iraq today

At the end of the last ice age, agriculture appeared in many different parts of the world at roughly the same time. Some archaeologists wonder if this is because annuals became common during this same time period due to Earth's changing climate.

Annuals are plants that grow, flower, and die in just one season, but they leave behind seeds for the following year. Annuals such as wheat, barley, peas, and lentils were the first crops human beings planted.

What do you think is the most important technology human beings ever developed?

For almost 200,000 years, human beings survived by hunting and gathering. They were **nomads** who traveled across the land, following herds of animals that provided them with meat. These early human beings also **foraged** for plants wherever they went. Neither the people nor the animals settled anywhere for long, though. Once all the **edible** plants in an area were eaten, or disappeared because the seasons changed, the herds moved on and human beings followed right behind them.

Then, about 10,000 years ago, human beings discovered how to save the seeds of certain plants and use them to grow crops. Human beings no longer had to move constantly from place to place. The **Neolithic Age**, and human civilization, arrived with the beginning of agriculture.

Agriculture may be the most important process that human beings ever developed. Earlier human beings had carved tools from stone to help them hunt. They had learned to control fire so they could cook their food and scare away predators. Early human beings had even cleared the land to make hunting easier and to give the wild plants they ate more room to grow. But none of these developments allowed human beings to settle in one place.

Agriculture meant controlling nature at a much higher level. In order to grow crops, human beings had to understand how to get the soil ready for planting, which seeds would grow into edible plants, how to water and weed the fields, and how to gather and store seeds for the following year's crops. No one knows for sure how this knowledge was learned, but it seems to have appeared in many different parts of the world at almost the same time.

The earliest signs of agriculture have been found in **Mesopotamia** and Egypt. Both of these areas benefited from major rivers that flooded the land each year. These floods soaked the soil with important nutrients and made it perfect for growing crops year after year.

The change from hunting and gathering to growing crops didn't happen overnight. If crops failed, groups probably returned to hunting and gathering for a season or two before trying again. The ability to grow crops, though, meant that human beings could settle in one place. New skills and occupations arose once people didn't have to spend all their time searching for food.

Circle the letter of the best answer to each question below.

1. The earliest signs of agriculture have been found in

   a. North America.

   b. the Middle East.

   c. Australia.

   d. South America.

2. The first human beings were

   a. hunter-gatherers.

   b. nomads.

   c. foragers.

   d. All of the above

Write your answers on the lines below.

3. Was agriculture the first example of human beings controlling nature? Explain your answer.

   _____

   _____

4. What characteristic do annuals have that led them to become the first plants grown by

   early farmers?_____

5. The first farm animals were domesticated, or tamed, at about the same time that human beings discovered agriculture. How did this change also allow human beings to settle down?

   _____

   _____

   _____

What's Next?

Mesopotamia is often called the *cradle of civilization*. Why was it so important in human history, and what historical event does Mesopotamia have in common with Egypt, the Indus Valley in India, and the Yellow River Valley in China?

From China to the Moon

internal combustion engine: an engine that is powered by the energy of explosions; the explosions occur when mixtures of gasoline and air are ignited

exhaust: gas that leaves an engine

nozzle: a short tube that becomes narrower on one end

Many of Nazi Germany's top scientists were secretly brought to the United States at the end of World War II in a program called *Operation Paperclip*. Some military and political leaders thought their knowledge of rockets and nuclear power would be useful in the Cold War that was just beginning with the Soviet Union.

Missiles are military rockets that carry explosives to their targets.

What gives a rocket its power?

World War II raged across Europe, and British citizens understood the drill. When they heard buzzing engines overhead, it was time to seek shelter quickly. German bombs were about to fall. The buzzing didn't come from airplanes, though. It was the engines of V-1 flying bombs. They were unmanned jets rushing to blow up their targets.

Then, in 1944, Londoners suddenly lost their warning. There was only silence before each deadly explosion. The Germans had created the V-2 rocket, which moved faster than the speed of sound.

Germans didn't invent rockets, and they weren't the first to use them as weapons either. About 2,000 years ago in China, simple rockets were first used as fireworks. Gunpowder was placed inside a tube that had been sealed at one end. When the gunpowder was lit, the force of the explosion blew out the open end and propelled the tube forward.

Rocket technology is based on Newton's Third Law of Motion: Every action has an equal and opposite reaction. Most rockets use an **internal combustion engine**. A powerful chemical reaction inside the engine produces an explosion. The **exhaust** from this explosion blows out of a narrow opening at one end of the rocket. The force of the exhaust creates an equal and opposite force that pushes the rocket forward.

Rocket technology slowly spread from China to Europe. These early rockets were very inefficient and inaccurate, though. During the 1800s, engineers found rocket shapes that flew with much greater precision, but the engines still wasted a lot of energy.

Around 1920, Robert Goddard attached a **nozzle** to the bottom of a rocket. Forcing exhaust through the nozzle's narrow opening created a tremendous amount of thrust. Rocket engines became much more efficient.

By the late 1930s, Nazi scientists had designed the most powerful rocket yet, the V-2. It zoomed into the thermosphere, cruised toward its target, and then dove back toward Earth at hundreds of miles per hour.

After World War II, many of Germany's top scientists ended up in the United States. Their knowledge of rocketry was put to use in the space program. Soon, rockets launched satellites and spacecraft into orbit around Earth, and eventually sent people to the moon.

Circle the letter of the best answer to each question below.

1. Rockets were first developed

   a. in Germany in the 1930s.

   b. in the United States after World War II.

   c. 2,000 years ago in China.

   d. during the 1800s in Europe.

2. A missile is

   a. a rocket that uses liquid fuel.

   b. a rocket that carries an explosive.

   c. different than a rocket because it uses a motor.

   d. an advanced type of rocket that uses a nozzle.

Write your answers on the lines below.

3. Why didn't British citizens know when a V-2 rocket was about to hit?

   _____

4. Using Newton's Third Law of Motion, explain how a rocket moves forward.

   _____

   _____

Unifying Concepts and Processes

1. What happens if you partially block the stream of water coming out of a hose? Use your answer to describe in detail why a nozzle makes a rocket more efficient.

   _____

   _____

   _____

2. Rockets need thrust in order to fly, but does it always need to be created by an explosion? Explain your answer.

   _____

   _____

The AC/DC Battle: Tesla Versus Edison

transformer: a device that increases or decreases the voltage of an electrical current

Electricity can be measured in amps and volts. An easy way to understand the difference between them is to imagine water flowing through a hose. Volts measure how much pressure the water creates as it pushes through the hose. Amps measure the water's speed as it flows through the hose. Volts measure how much power, or force, an electrical current has, and amps measure how fast it travels.

In the U.S., nearly all homes have 120 volts of AC electricity flowing from their outlets. The amps change depending on the device being used.

A battery creates an electrical current that flows in one direction through a device, which means that battery-powered devices use DC electricity.

What kind of electrical current flows into your home?

Thomas Edison was involved with the invention of many technologies during the late 1800s. It's no surprise, then, that he also helped create a system for supplying electricity to all those new devices. The first large, electric power plant was built and operated by Edison in New York City. It opened for business in 1882 and created a huge amount of electricity.

Edison's system used direct current, or DC, electricity. The electrons in a direct current move in a single direction through a wire. Edison's power plant created DC electricity and sent it into the surrounding neighborhoods. People living near the plant had plenty of power, but after traveling about a mile through wires, DC electricity loses a lot of its power. In order to provide enough electricity for an entire city, dozens of Edison's DC power plants needed to be built.

One of Edison's employees, a man named Nikola Tesla, had been experimenting with alternating currents, or AC electricity. The electrons in an AC current don't move in just one direction. They quickly switch directions back and forth inside the wire. Tesla knew that a **transformer** could be used to make the AC electricity extremely powerful. It could then be sent long distances, even hundreds of miles, without losing any of its strength. When AC electricity reached its destination, another transformer made it less powerful again so that it could be used for lights and other low-power devices.

AC electricity was more efficient, but Edison was convinced DC power was the answer. He thought it was safer. DC power remained at safe, low levels as it traveled from the power plant to the neighborhoods.

Tesla quit in frustration, and several years later went to work for Edison's main competitor, George Westinghouse. With Westinghouse's money, Tesla developed an AC power system that quickly demonstrated its advantages over DC. For example, a single massive power plant could be built outside a city instead of having power plants all over the place. Devices that needed more or less power could be used because a transformer would boost or reduce the electricity as needed. In Edison's DC system, all devices had to use the same, low level of electricity.

Over time, Edison's DC plants gave way to Tesla's AC power. Today, all over the world, AC powers the devices in homes and businesses.

NAME _____

Circle the letter of the best answer to each question below.

1. What role did transformers play in Tesla's AC electrical system?

   a. They were used instead of wires to carry electricity.

   b. They changed the voltage of electrical currents.

   c. They changed DC electricity into AC electricity.

   d. They blocked electrical currents that were unsafe.

2. DC electricity was inefficient for large-scale use because

   a. it lost power when it was sent over long distances.

   b. only small amounts could be made each day.

   c. the plants needed to be extremely large to produce enough power.

   d. Both a and c

Write your answers on the lines below.

3. Briefly describe the difference between alternating and direct currents.

   _____

   _____

4. Many battery-powered devices come with cords that allow them to be plugged into electrical outlets. What change has to take place inside the power cord in order for the device to function properly?

   _____

Wattage is determined by multiplying the voltage times the amperage (volts x amps = watts). For example, a 240-watt device plugged into a 120-volt outlet uses 2 amps of electricity, or 120 X 2 = 240. Use the formula above to answer the following questions.

5. How many amps does a 60-watt light bulb use when it's powered by 120 volts? _____

6. What wattage is a toaster that uses 5 amps from a 120-volt outlet? _____

7. Clothes dryers need special plugs that provide a higher voltage than most other common appliances. How many volts does the outlet provide for a 4,800-watt dryer that uses 20 amps of power?

   _____

A Picture Is Worth a Thousand Sounds

ultrasound: sound waves that are smaller, or of a higher frequency, than can be heard by human beings

echolocation: a method of using sound waves to locate and identify objects

probe: a medical or scientific tool used for investigating

two-dimensional: something flat that exists in two directions, height and width

three-dimensional: something solid that exists in three directions, height, width, and depth

Sonar is similar to ultrasound, but it sends out large sound waves—ones that human beings can hear—to create images based on returning echoes. Submarines and boats use sonar to find objects underwater.

Radar emits radio waves and then reads how the waves echo back after hitting objects within the radar's range. Radar is used to "see" objects like airplanes, cloud formations, and landforms.

How can ultrasound see inside our bodies?

During a humid summer night, you see a huge fork of lightning fill the sky. You begin counting the seconds. When you reach five, thunder rattles through the air. You know that the lightning struck about one mile away, because sound waves travel about one mile every five seconds, or about 720 miles per hour. You just used sound to measure distance, something many scientists and doctors do all the time using **ultrasound** technology.

All sound moves as waves through gases, solids, and liquids. These waves come in a wide range of sizes, but human hearing is limited to sound waves that fall within a certain range. For example, ultrasound waves have a frequency too high for human beings to hear. Bats and dolphins, though, use them to "see" the world in a process called **echolocation**. In a similar way, people use ultrasound to make images of things we can't see with our eyes.

If you yell into a small canyon, the echo will return quickly because it had only a short distance to travel. In a larger canyon, the echo will return more slowly because it had farther to travel. Ultrasound technology sends out pulses of sound waves and then measures how long each one takes to return. Then, it uses the information to create an image.

Doctors can use ultrasound to see inside our bodies. A **probe** held against a patient's skin acts like both a speaker and a microphone. It emits millions of ultrasound waves per second into the patient's body, and then reads the echoes that bounce back. As these pulses move through the body, they bounce off the denser layers found between soft tissues and return to the probe as echoes. The ultrasound machine measures the distance each pulse travels before it returns to the probe. Then it uses these measurements to construct an image that appears on a computer screen.

Most ultrasounds are **two-dimensional**, but recent technology has been developed that allows a **three-dimensional** picture to be made from a combination of many 2-D images.

Compared to X-rays, which use a form of radiation, ultrasound is much safer. It's commonly used to see babies growing inside pregnant women with little risk to the health of the mother or unborn child. Ultrasound waves can create heat, and there is a very small risk of damaging tissues, but the benefits of getting a view inside our bodies without surgery or radiation outweigh the risks.

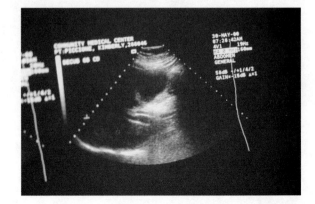

Circle the letter of the best answer to each question below.

1. What is ultrasound?

   a. a machine that creates sound waves

   b. the way bats and dolphins "see"

   c. sound that human beings can't hear

   d. sound waves that have echoed off an object

2. What is the probe used for in ultrasound technology?

   a. emitting sound waves

   b. receiving sound waves

   c. creating ultrasound

   d. All of the above

3. Three-dimensional ultrasound images are made by

   a. using special ultrasounds that are created by a laser.

   b. using echolocation.

   c. combining many different two-dimensional images.

   d. sending sound waves through solid materials instead of air.

Write your answers on the lines below.

4. What does an ultrasound machine measure?

   _____

5. Explain the similarities and differences between sonar and ultrasound.

   _____

   _____

6. Explain the similarities and differences between radar and ultrasound imaging.

   _____

   _____

7. Why are unborn babies viewed with ultrasound instead of X-rays?

   _____

trial and error: the process in which one learns by making mistakes, fixing them, and trying again

concentrated: located or placed in a small area

Dead load is the weight of the material used to construct something, like a bridge or a building. Live load is the temporary weight the structure supports. For a bridge, live load might be cars. In a skyscraper, it could be human beings and office equipment.

There are three major types of bridges:

- A beam bridge is a horizontal surface supported by a column on either end. It is weaker than other bridges and spans the least distance.

- An arch bridge is flat on top and supported below by material in the shape of a semicircle.

- A suspension bridge can span long distances. The road hangs from steel cables draped across towers. The cables are anchored in concrete at the ends of the bridge.

Is it possible to make a bridge out of paper?

"How's it going?" Ms. Darr asked. "What have you learned so far?"

"It's going pretty well," said Kirsten. "It's taken a bit of **trial and error**, but we've found a couple of sturdy bridge designs."

"We started out with two shoe boxes of the same size, which we placed six inches apart," said Diego. "We laid a piece of copy paper between the boxes and placed pieces of pasta on the paper to see how many our bridge could hold before collapsing."

"It could only hold three pieces of pasta," Anthony volunteered.

"How did you make your bridge stronger?" asked Ms. Darr.

"We tried several different designs," explained Kirsten. "First, we folded the paper four times so that it was thicker but narrower. It could support more weight because it was thicker, so it held 15 pieces of pasta."

"Did you place all the pasta in the center of the bridge, or did you space it out?" asked Ms. Darr.

"It was spaced out in the second bridge, but **concentrated** in the center on the first bridge," replied Diego. "Maybe we should make the first bridge again and spread out the pasta to see if it makes a difference."

"That would limit your variables," agreed Ms. Darr.

"We rolled the paper into a tube, fastened each end together with a paper clip, and placed the pasta inside," said Diego. "The tube was stronger. It didn't collapse, but after about 20 pieces, the tube became distorted and changed shape. Next, we used a second piece of paper to create an arch beneath the folded-paper bridge. That increased its strength and allowed it to hold 25 pieces of pasta."

"The last bridge we made was the strongest," said Anthony. "We folded the paper accordion-style, and then stacked the pasta across the peaks. By the time we reached 58 pieces, the pasta became too difficult to stack. This bridge never collapsed, and its shape didn't become distorted at all."

"Excellent job!" said Ms. Darr.

Circle the letter of the best answer to the question below.

1. Based on the experiments in the selection, which of the following statements is true?

    a. A bridge can support the most weight when that weight is concentrated in one position.

    b. If you change the shape of a material, the way it resists a force, like weight, also changes.

    c. The bridge the students built using two sheets of paper was a suspension bridge.

    d. Both a and b

Write your answers on the lines below.

2. Think of another bridge design the students could test. Tell whether your design would be stronger or weaker than the designs in the selection, and explain why.

    _____

    _____

    _____

3. Is a piece of corrugated cardboard (shown in the photo on page 96) stronger or weaker than a plain piece of cardboard? Why?

    _____

4. Does changing the distance between the boxes have any effect on the outcome of the experiment?

    _____

    _____

5. The image above shows a truss bridge. Which of the bridges that the students built uses a similar concept? What element of this type of bridge do you think offers the most support?

    _____

    _____

tunnel: an underground passageway used by pedestrians, vehicles, power lines, water, or sewage

aqueducts: structures that carry large amounts of moving water

tunnel-boring machine: also called a *mole*; a machine that uses blades to cut and grind rock in the construction of a tunnel

A mole can drill an average of 250 feet of tunnel per day.

The Chunnel is a 31-mile long rail tunnel that lies below the English Channel and connects England and France. It cost $16 billion to build, and took 13,000 workers seven years to complete. There are two tubes for rail traffic and a third, smaller tube that is used as a service tunnel and emergency escape route.

How are tunnels through mountains constructed?

You may not realize it, but networks of tunnels wind their way underground all over the world. A **tunnel** is an underground passage that may be used for car or boat traffic, subways, pedestrians, water or sewage, or power and communication lines. Some of the earliest tunnels were the Roman **aqueducts**. They were used to carry clean water into cities and transport sewage away. Even without electric machinery, the Romans constructed tunnels that lasted into modern times.

With the invention of cars, more tunnels were needed. Although they are more expensive to build than bridges, sometimes tunnels are the better choice. For example, a tunnel is the only way to get from one side of a mountain to the other without going over or around it. An underwater tunnel doesn't interfere with boat traffic the way a bridge might. In addition, as cities get more crowded, going underground is a practical option.

The method used to create a tunnel depends on where it is to be constructed and what material will surround it. A tunnel through mountain rock is usually made with a **tunnel-boring machine**, or mole. This powerful machine is shaped like a large cylinder. It cuts and grinds through rock, leaving behind a passageway. Because rock surrounds the tunnel, extra support isn't necessary during construction. Explosives were used before the invention of moles, but moles are safer and quieter. They also leave behind a smoother tunnel of the exact shape the engineers want.

Building an underwater tunnel is very different. The ground is soft and waterlogged, so the builders need support to prevent collapse. A metallic shield with sharp edges is used to cut through the ground. It also provides support while the workers construct the actual tunnel inside it.

A tube is another option for underwater construction. First, a deep trench is dug underwater. Pieces of the tunnel that were built on land are sunk in place, attached to one another, and then drained. The tunnel is usually covered with heavy materials, like concrete, to protect it and weigh it down.

Engineers have come up with all kinds of creative solutions for underground problems they encounter. For example, during the "Big Dig," a 3.5-mile tunnel below the city of Boston, engineers had to find a way to deal with the loose, soggy soil. Their solution? They froze it to make it solid and easier to move!

Circle the letter of the best answer to each question below.

1. The Chunnel is

   a. the first tunnel built by the Romans.

   b. a bridge that connects England and France.

   c. an underwater rail tunnel that connects England and France.

   d. an English tunnel used for boat traffic.

2. What kind of material is a tunnel-boring machine used to tunnel through?

   a. rock

   b. soft soil

   c. sandy soil

   d. Both b and c

Write **true** or **false** next to each statement below.

3. _____ The passage through which a subway travels is a tunnel.

4. _____ Moles are usually used for digging underwater tunnels.

5. _____ An immersed tube would most likely be used when building a tunnel through a mountain.

6. _____ Tunnels are often more expensive to construct than bridges are, but sometimes they are a more practical choice.

Write your answers on the lines below.

7. What was the purpose of the Roman aqueducts?

   _____

8. Why do you think loose, soggy soil was a problem for workers on the Big Dig? How did they deal with it?

   _____

   _____

9. Give two reasons why builders would prefer using moles to drilling and using explosives.

   _____

   _____

Up, Up, and Away!

altitude: the vertical height of something above a surface, such as the ground

envelope: the part of the balloon that contains the heated gas

propane: a flammable gas often used as fuel in engines and grills

Each cubic foot of air in a hot air balloon has the power to lift about 7 grams, which is only about a quarter of an ounce. To lift 1,000 pounds, you'd need about 65,000 cubic feet of air.

Helium and hydrogen are two other gases that are often used in balloons. Hydrogen is flammable (meaning that it catches fire easily), so helium is a safer choice.

Today, balloons are popular tools of scientific research. They can be used to take measurements in the atmosphere and can even carry telescopes used for astronomical observation.

How do hot air balloons work?

In 1250, British scientist Roger Bacon described a flying machine made of a thin metal globe filled with what he called *liquid fire*. No one was quite sure how to make a working model, but over the next few centuries, various people experimented with ideas for human flight. The key was to fill the globe with something lighter than air, which would allow the vehicle to float. Two French brothers, Joseph and Étienne Montgolfier, believed that if they could find the right special gas, their balloon would fly.

In 1783, the Montgolfier brothers put their idea to the test with live animals. The passengers in their linen-and-paper balloon were a duck, a rooster, and a sheep. They wanted to see whether the animals could breathe at a high **altitude**. In front of King Louis XVI and thousands of onlookers, the Montgolfier brothers lit a fire in their balloon. The tethered balloon, attached to the ground with ropes, rose to a height of about 1,700 feet and traveled about two miles. Eight minutes later, the animals and the balloon returned safely to the ground.

The Montgolfiers didn't actually create a special gas, they just heated the air inside the balloon. When air is heated, it expands. The excited molecules move around, taking up more space. Some air escapes from the mouth of the balloon, leaving fewer atoms inside the **envelope**, or the bag. Because the hot air is less dense than the cooler air outside the balloon, the balloon rises.

Today, fire using wood and straw does not heat the air in a balloon. Instead, a gas called **propane** is often used to create heat. Unlike using fire, the pilot can control propane tanks by turning them off and on. When a pilot wants to descend, he or she pulls a cord and opens the parachute valve at the top of the envelope. This allows some of the hot air to escape, causing the balloon to sink.

Pilots have some, but not much, control over the path a balloon takes. The wind blows in different directions at different altitudes. By changing the balloon's altitude, the pilot can catch a wind current that is moving in the direction he or she wants to go.

Circle the letter of the best answer to each question below.

1. A parachute valve

   a. allows a pilot to make a quick escape if necessary.

   b. is located beside the propane tanks.

   c. allows hot air to escape, which causes the balloon to descend.

   d. allows the pilot to ascend, or rise, quickly into the air.

2. Why does hot air cause a balloon to rise?

   a. Cool air is less dense than hot air.

   b. Hot air is less dense than cool air.

   c. When air is heated, it is converted into a very light gas.

   d. Hot air doesn't cause a balloon to rise; a special gas does.

Write your answers on the lines below.

3. Why did the Montgolfier brothers send three animals up in their balloon?

   _____

4. In your own words, explain how a pilot of a hot air balloon can change direction.

   _____

   _____

5. Why do you think that traveling by hot air balloon isn't a very efficient way to get from place to place?

   _____

6. Why does using propane as a source of heat rather than fire give the pilot more control over the balloon?

   _____

   _____

Unifying Concepts and Processes

What does something that floats in water have in common with something that floats in the air?

_____

At the Bottom of the Ocean

bathysphere: a steel sphere used for exploring deep underwater

porthole: a small, circular window in a ship or aircraft

submersible: an underwater craft often used for deep-sea research

Many interesting creatures have been encountered during *Alvin's* voyages, such eight-foot-long tubeworms with no mouths and Pompeii worms that can survive at temperatures of 176°F.

Japan's *Shinkai 6500* is the world's deepest-diving submersible. It can reach a depth of 6,500 meters, or 21,325 feet.

What are some of Alvin's *discoveries?*

For years, the deep waters of the oceans were completely unknown to human beings. Then, in the early 1930s, explorers William Beebe and Otis Barton created the **bathysphere**. It was an enormous steel ball equipped with oxygen tanks that could be lowered deep into the water by a cable extended from a boat. It allowed the men to travel more than 3,000 feet underwater. As they peered out the **porthole**, they encountered all kinds of new life forms.

Since that time, technology has come a long way. Even so, the best American **submersible** we have today, *Alvin*, was actually built in 1964. It has had lots of updates since then, though, and every single part has been replaced. It is also completely taken apart every three to five years and to make sure that everything is in good working order.

During its lifetime, *Alvin* has made more than 4,200 dives. It can travel nearly 15,000 feet deep, which is almost 3 miles underwater. The conditions inside *Alvin* are fairly cramped. There is room for only two scientists and a pilot. Trips usually last about eight hours, and two to four hours of that are travel time. Although *Alvin* is a high-tech research instrument, it uses a pretty low-tech method for descending to the ocean floor. Four steel weights drag the vehicle down. When the pilot wants to return to the surface, he or she just releases the weights.

Once they reach their destination, the scientists begin gathering data. They use digital cameras to take photos and videos of the deep-sea environment. Sunlight does not reach below a depth of about 3,000 feet, so the sub must use its powerful searchlights to illuminate the surroundings.

The researchers aren't able to exit the sub at such great depths because the pressure is too intense. With computers, the scientists are able to use *Alvin's* robotic arms, or manipulators, to gather samples of rocks, mud, life forms, and water. The samples are placed in a large basket that can hold up to 1,500 pounds.

Alvin has allowed human beings to journey to places they could never see without the use of technology. What new discovery do you think *Alvin* will help human beings make next?

Use the words in the box to complete the sentences below.

porthole	manipulators	pressure	submersible

1. The bathysphere was an early example of a _____.

2. Scientists observe life deep under water by looking through a _____.

3. *Alvin's* cameras and _____ help scientists gather data.

4. Intense _____ prevents scientists from leaving a sub at great depths.

Write your answers on the lines below.

5. Explain how *Alvin* descends to the floor of the ocean and then returns to the surface.

   _____

   _____

6. How is a deep-sea submersible similar to a spacecraft?

   _____

   _____

7. Why do you think such thorough checks of all *Alvin's* parts are done every few years?

   _____

   _____

8. What service do *Alvin's* manipulators perform for the scientists onboard? Why are the manipulators necessary?

   _____

   _____

Unifying Concepts and Processes

Do you think that studying life on the ocean floor could help scientists determine if there is life on other planets? Explain your answer.

_____

_____

nanorobots: robots that are built and operated at the molecular level

nanotechnology: the science of controlling and building materials at the atomic or molecular level

nanoscale: a scale of measurement that ranges from 1 to 100 nanometers

proteins: substances that contain carbon, hydrogen, oxygen, and nitrogen, and that are essential for life

microchips: tiny groups of electrical devices on a slice of silicon

film: thin skin or membrane

etched: produced lines or patterns on a hard surface by eating away at the material

Nanorobots don't quite exist yet. Scientists are still experimenting with ways to give energy and motion to matter built at the nanoscale. For now, nanotechnology has been most successful in creating chemicals that are used in things like sunscreens, clothing, and paints.

How small is the smallest machine?

In the last few years, **nanorobots** have become popular features in fictional books, films, and cartoons. These tiny devices aren't total science fiction, though. Scientists in the field of **nanotechnology** have found ways to create machines at the molecular level.

The prefix *nano-* means "billionth." In nanotechnology, the main unit of measurement is the nanometer, which is one billionth of a meter. A human hair, for example, is about 30,000 nanometers wide.

Although atoms are only about one-tenth of one nanometer wide, the other building blocks of nature fall into the **nanoscale**, meaning they are somewhere between 1 and 100 nanometers in size. This includes the individual molecules of **proteins**, viruses, and many drugs.

The ability to work at such a small scale is exciting for many scientists. Designing new molecules, particles, and even simple machines at the atomic level opens up a new world of technologies. For example, tiny human-made particles might be able to break up the chemicals in an oil spill. They might enter a cell and destroy the molecules of a deadly virus.

The electron microscope is an important tool for the nanoscientist. The beams of electrons that scan objects to magnify them can be used in a similar way to move around single atoms and molecules. Electrical charges that attract or repel other charges can push or pull atoms into place. Building molecules or other matter one atom at a time is known as the *bottom-up approach* in nanotechnology.

The top-down approach begins with a much bigger piece of matter that is carved down. Computer **microchips** are made this way. They begin as tiny squares of silicon covered by a **film**. The film is **etched** away until all that remains of it are thin pathways running across the silicon chip. These pathways carry the electrical current that makes the chip useful. Most chips aren't small enough to be measured on the nanoscale, but the top-down approach is used to manufacture many other kinds of nanotechnology.

Nanoscientists hope to produce a nanorobot someday that can make copies of itself. What if populations of these tiny machines get out of control? Critics say they could upset nature's delicate balance, but nanoscientists argue that the reproduction would be carefully controlled. What do you think?

Circle the letter of the best answer to each question below.

1. The prefix *nano-* means

   a. "tiny."

   b. "microscopic."

   c. "billionth."

   d. "robotic."

2. How wide is an atom?

   a. less than one nanometer

   b. several nanometers

   c. thousands of nanometers

   d. one millimeter

3. Which of the following statements is true?

   a. All computer microchips are built at the nanoscale.

   b. All computer microchips are larger than the nanoscale.

   c. Most computer microchips are built at the nanoscale.

   d. A few computer microchips are built at the nanoscale.

Write your answers on the lines below.

4. Briefly describe the top-down method used in nanotechnology.

   _____

   _____

5. Now, briefly describe the bottom-up method.

   _____

   _____

6. During the Industrial Revolution 200 years ago, steam power, machines, and factories were introduced and changed the world dramatically. Some scientists think nanotechnology could have the same effect. What do you think?

   _____

   _____

Review

Circle the letter of the best answer to each question below.

1. What did Robert Goddard attach to rockets to make them more efficient?

    a. internal combustion engines

    b. fins

    c. nozzles

    d. wings

2. Why is exploring the deep sea similar to exploring space?

    a. Human beings need special equipment to survive the extreme conditions.

    b. There are still many mysteries left to be discovered.

    c. Human beings hope to someday live in both places.

    d. Both a and b

3. What is the bottom-up approach in nanotechnology?

    a. carving molecular-sized materials with a laser

    b. building molecular-sized materials one atom at a time

    c. cutting molecular-sized materials from the undersides of silicon chips

    d. creating microchips from silicon

Write your answers on the lines below.

4. Briefly explain how agriculture advanced civilization.

    _____

    _____

5. Why can it be said that agriculture is the most important technology human beings ever developed?

    _____

6. Explain how rockets use Newton's third law of motion to move.

    _____

    _____

7. Why did Edison think AC electricity was a bad idea?

    _____

8. Why can't human beings hear ultrasound?

_____

9. Briefly describe how an ultrasound machine creates images.

_____

10. In the selection about building a paper bridge, what did the students do to the paper to increase the weight the bridge could bear?

_____

11. Describe two uses of tunnels other than for vehicles.

_____

12. Why are moles preferred over explosives for building tunnels?

_____

13. Why does the hot air inside a balloon cause the balloon to rise into the cooler air above?

_____

14. Why do deep-sea submersibles need to be equipped with powerful lights?

_____

15. What is one way that nanotechnology is being used today?

_____

Underline the correct answer from the two choices you are given.

16. Before agriculture, human beings (foraged, traded) for the food they needed to survive.

17. The (fuel, exhaust) shooting out of a rocket propels it forward.

18. Electrical appliances that plug into outlets use (AC, DC) electricity.

19. An electrical current's speed is measured in (watts, amps).

20. (Radar, sonar) uses radio waves to locate objects and create images of them.

21. Modern hot air balloons use (methane, propane) fuel as the source of their heat.

22. The materials used to build a bridge are considered to be the (live, dead) load.

23. A nanometer is one (millionth, billionth) of a meter.

Lesson 6.1	Counting Calories

calorie: the unit used to measure the potential energy in a food

empty calories: calories that come from foods that have little or no nutritional value

Fast food can quickly sneak more calories into your diet. A cheeseburger and medium French fries have almost 800 calories. That is about a third of the calories you should consume in an entire day.

A calorie, called a *kilocalorie* in scientific terms, is the amount of energy needed to heat one kilogram of water 1°C.

What exactly does a calorie measure?

Do you know how many calories a peach has? What about a pork chop, a piece of chocolate cake, a green pepper, or a corn tortilla? A **calorie** (Cal) is the unit used to measure the potential energy in a food. Foods are made of three main parts: carbohydrates, proteins, and fats. A gram of carbohydrate and a gram of protein each have four calories, and a gram of fat has nine calories. The combination of these three elements gives you a total calorie count for a serving of food.

You may have heard people talk about "burning" calories. Everything you do burns calories, even breathing, yawning, or walking across the room to get a glass of water. The harder your body has to work, the more calories you burn. For a 90-pound child, riding a bike burns about 290 calories per hour, playing soccer burns around 250 calories, and swimming laps burns about 370 calories.

For the most part, healthy kids don't need to count calories in the foods they eat. If you eat a well-balanced diet, avoid sugary snacks, and are physically active most days of the week, you're probably eating the right amount of calories for your body. Remember, your body needs the energy in calories to function. When you eat too many calories, though, the extra calories are converted into fat and stored in your body. Occasionally eating more calories than you need isn't a problem. However, regularly eating more calories than your body needs can quickly add up. Consuming 500 extra calories a day can add up to a weight gain of one pound per week.

Eating **empty calories** is one way to get more calories than you need. Empty calories come from foods that aren't particularly nutritious or filling. A can of soda contains between 130 and 200 calories. The calories come from sugar, and there are no nutritional benefits to drinking soda.

How do you know how many calories a day you should eat? Most 12-year-olds need an average of between 2,200 and 2,500 calories per day. To find the exact number, you need to take several factors into account. Height, weight, age, gender, and activity level all play a part. Someone who plays sports, walks to school, and enjoys dancing and roller-blading as hobbies will need more calories than someone who spends a lot of time watching TV, surfing the Internet, and playing video games.

Circle the letter of the best answer to the question below.

1. You can figure out the amount of calories a food has if you know the amount of

    _____ it contains.

    a. proteins, fats, and carbohydrates

    b. fats and proteins

    c. vitamins, carbohydrates, and fats

    d. vitamins, minerals, and carbohydrates

Write your answers on the lines below.

2. What do calories measure?

    _____

    _____

3. Why does eating more calories than your body needs cause you to gain weight?

    _____

    _____

4. Why do you think that activity level is important to consider when you are figuring out how many calories your body needs a day?

    _____

    _____

5. Number the following activities from 1 to 4 to show which burns the most and least calories. (One is the least, and four is the most.)

    _____ typing at the computer   _____ playing hockey   _____ sleeping   _____ walking

What's Next?

It's good to know how many calories your body needs because it can help you make healthy choices. Do some research online or at the library to determine how many calories you need a day. Remember, though, that you should never try to lose weight without talking to your parents and your doctor.

vitamins: natural substances found in food that the body needs to grow and maintain health

mineral: small amounts of a metallic element that help the body's organs and systems function

fortified: containing added material for health

The nutritional information on prepackaged foods provides information about the calories, fat, fiber, and carbohydrates in each serving. It also shows how much of the recommended daily allowance (RDA) for each vitamin a serving contains.

Scurvy, the result of not getting enough Vitamin C, is a condition that affects the gums, sight, skin, and muscles. Scurvy was often seen in sailors who would go for long periods without eating fresh fruits and vegetables. In 1747, a Scottish surgeon found that citrus fruits could prevent scurvy. The use of lemons and limes by the British Navy caused the sailors to be nicknamed *limeys*.

What role do vitamins play in having a healthy body?

Do you ever eat something because it's full of **vitamins**? Vitamins are natural substances that are found in food. Your body needs vitamins to function and to grow. Eating a balanced diet is important because different foods contain different vitamins. If you eat lots of colorful foods and you cover all the food groups, your body should receive plenty of the vitamins it needs to grow and stay healthy.

Scientists divide the 13 major vitamins into two categories: water-soluble and fat-soluble. Water-soluble vitamins, vitamin C and all the B vitamins, don't get stored in your body for long. Whatever you don't use leaves your body in urine. You need to make sure that you eat foods containing these vitamins on a regular basis. Fat-soluble vitamins, vitamins A, D, E, and K, can be stored in your body's fat for days, or sometimes even months.

- Vitamin A is important in keeping your eyes healthy. It helps you see in color and see well at night. Vitamin A is also key to having healthy skin. Carrots, spinach, eggs, milk, cheese, and liver are good sources.

- The B vitamins help make red blood cells. They are also important in creating and releasing energy in your body and in the functioning of the nervous system. Eating foods like leafy green vegetables, dairy products, seafood, chicken, whole grains, and berries can provide your body with the different vitamin Bs.

- Vitamin C plays a role in the health of your bones and teeth. It also helps your body fight infections and heal itself. Vitamin C is found in citrus fruits, strawberries, cantaloupe, broccoli, and tomatoes.

- Vitamin D is also important in forming healthy bones and teeth. It helps your body use the **mineral** *calcium*, which is why products like milk (which is high in calcium) are usually **fortified** with Vitamin D. Vitamin D is the only vitamin that is also created in the body. Dairy products, eggs, and tuna are good sources.

- Vitamin E plays a role in forming red blood cells and keeping your body's tissues healthy. It is found in vegetable oils, leafy green vegetables, nuts, and whole grains.

- Vitamin K helps your blood clot when you get a cut. It's found in leafy green vegetables, dairy products, and liver.

Circle the letter of the best answer to the question below.

1. Which vitamin plays an important role in healthy bones and teeth?

   a. Vitamin D

   b. Vitamin C

   c. Vitamin K

   d. Both a and b

Write your answers on the lines below.

2. Explain the difference between water-soluble and fat-soluble vitamins.

   _____

   _____

3. Why did sailors often get scurvy? What other groups of people might be at risk for scurvy today?

   _____

   _____

4. Give examples of four foods that are good sources of at least two vitamins.

   _____   _____

   _____   _____

5. Why is it important to eat colorful foods and foods from different groups?

   _____

6. What is the RDA?

   _____

What's Next?

Milk isn't the only food that is fortified. In fact, many food companies try to make sure that their products offer as many health benefits as possible. The next time you go to the grocery store, pay attention to the labels you see on different kinds of food. What kinds of products are fortified? What other claims do companies make about the vitamins and minerals their products contain? If you compare the labels of those products with others, are there really any differences?

Standing Up to Earthquakes

earthquake-prone: likely to experience earthquakes

magnitude: the intensity of an earthquake

absorb: to receive or take in without giving back

flexibility: allows movement without snapping or breaking

When the Great San Francisco earthquake struck in 1906, it destroyed about 80% of the city. Measuring 7.8 on the Richter scale, it wasn't even one of the five largest quakes in history. Although the earthquake itself was severe, the fires that broke out afterward caused even more damage.

The Uniform Building Code is used to provide safety standards for buildings. Research that scientists and engineers do on buildings in earthquake-prone areas affects the building code. This usually isn't a problem for new buildings that are being built. It can be expensive, though, for older buildings to have changes made that will allow them to meet the code.

How can buildings be designed to resist the enormous strength of earthquakes?

Scientists and engineers have been working for years to make safer structures that are better at withstanding earthquakes. Some people use the term *earthquake-proof* to describe the latest structures, though *earthquake-resistant* is probably more appropriate. The main goal of the researchers is to make structures that won't collapse and put human lives in danger.

One way they learn about what changes need to be made is by studying buildings that have been damaged during a quake. Even badly damaged buildings give engineers information. Scientists can learn what kind of stress intense shaking puts on a building. Then, they can work to design buildings that don't have the same weaknesses.

Beginning in the 1940s, researchers installed instruments in and nearby buildings to measure how the buildings reacted to earthquakes. Gathering and analyzing this data allows the engineers to identify both the strengths and weaknesses of the buildings. Today, high-tech versions of these instruments are placed in skyscrapers, hospitals, dams, and bridges that are located in **earthquake-prone** areas.

At Lehigh University's Center for Advanced Technology for Large Structural Systems (ATLSS), scientists conduct research that might have a major impact on the safety of buildings during earthquakes. At the center, the force and intensity of the Great San Francisco Earthquake of 1906 is produced. The frame of a building, or parts of a structure, are tested to see how well they can stand up to the shaking at a high **magnitude**.

One technique involves keeping the base of the building separate from the shaking ground. Large pads, springs, or rollers can **absorb** some of the movement from the ground and keep all of it from being transferred to the building—think of it as shock absorbers for a building instead of a car.

In other studies, parts of the building's structure are given a little **flexibility** to move when the ground shakes. They are surrounded by steel bands that hold them in place once the shaking has stopped.

Although a true earthquake-proof building may be far off in the future, advances that are made every day make buildings safer and stronger in the face of a natural disaster.

Write **true** or **false** next to each statement below.

1. _____ Magnitude measures how long an earthquake lasts.

2. _____ Fires caused much of the damage during the San Francisco earthquake of 1906.

3. _____ Most buildings around the world are completely earthquake-proof.

4. _____ Few earthquakes take place in earthquake-prone areas of the world.

5. _____ Human beings are able to create forces that are similar to the forces created by an earthquake.

Write your answers on the lines below.

6. Why is *earthquake-resistant* a better way to describe modern buildings than *earthquake-proof*?

_____

_____

7. Why do you think it can be hard for older buildings to meet new safety standards?

_____

8. Imagine that a strong earthquake hits a major city. Several buildings are nearly destroyed. What can engineers learn from examining these buildings?

_____

_____

9. What is the purpose of placing springs or rollers beneath a building?

_____

10. How do you think scientists decide what types of structures they should place the measuring instruments in?

_____

11. Why is flexibility important in an earthquake-resistant building?

_____

Water: A Resource at Risk

hydrated: supplied with enough water

aquifers: layers of underground rock, sand, or gravel that hold water

droughts: long periods without rain

developing countries: nations with limited economic resources; they often receive aid from the wealthier nations of the world

poverty: lack of money or resources

Much of Earth's fresh water is used for manufacturing and farming. One of the biggest uses of water in agriculture is the production of beef. Each cow drinks nearly 50 gallons of water a day. Water is used to clean cattle, to grow the grain that feeds cattle, and it's used in the processing of beef. In all, more than 1,000 gallons of water go into producing a single hamburger.

Almost 40 percent of America's rivers are too polluted for swimming or fishing.

Is a water crisis sweeping our planet?

After air, water is the most vital substance we need to survive. We can live for weeks without food, but only days without water. More than half of our bodies are water, and we need at least two quarts of water daily to stay **hydrated**. We also use it to cook, bathe, and wash clothes.

Water covers more than two-thirds of Earth's surface, but nearly all of it is salt water in the oceans. Only three percent of Earth's water is fresh water. Two-thirds of that fresh water is frozen in the polar ice caps and glaciers, though, which means that only one percent of Earth's water is thawed, drinkable fresh water. It's found in lakes, rivers, and underground **aquifers**, and in Earth's atmosphere as rain and clouds.

The supply of fresh water is already naturally limited, but it is even more limited in places where the water has become too polluted to use. **Droughts** can make the situation even worse because pollutants become more concentrated in lower water levels. Floods aren't much better, though, because they sweep additional garbage and pollution into the water supply.

Access to clean water may be the biggest global crisis we have right now. Almost one out of five people around the world lacks safe drinking water. This problem occurs most often in **developing countries**, but it can happen anywhere there is **poverty**, even in the United States.

Water treatment plants are expensive, and some countries don't have the resources to build them. People have to spend hours every day walking to collect water. This means they don't have time to go to school or earn a living doing other work.

Two out of every five people in the world also lack sewage systems that remove and clean their waste. People, especially babies, can become extremely sick, and even die, from drinking water that contains the bacteria living in human waste.

However, in the last 20 years, the global water crisis has caught the world's attention. Leaders are looking for ways to solve this complex problem. In the United States, water use has actually decreased since the 1970s because of better technology and laws that help reduce wastefulness.

We can all help to conserve this precious resource. Turn off the water while you brush your teeth or wash dishes. Take shorter showers and fix leaky faucets. Water is the liquid of life—treat it with care.

Circle the letter of the best answer to the question below.

1. Only three percent of Earth's water is

   a. found in the oceans.

   b. not salt water.

   c. found in the polar ice caps.

   d. Both b and c

Write your answers on the lines below.

2. Not having access to clean water can lead to other social problems, such as increased poverty and a lack of education. Why?

   _____

   _____

3. Explain how droughts can make water pollution worse.

   _____

   _____

4. Although sewage dumped into rivers, streams, and lakes seems like an obvious source of pollution, solid waste can be just as harmful. How do you think garbage buried in a landfill can be a source of pollution in the water supply?

   _____

   _____

5. In the 1990s, laws were passed that required all toilets in the United States to use less water. Today, toilets are very efficient. They use a lot less water per flush, but have no problem doing the job they were designed to do. Do you think it's right for the government to pass laws that limit the amount of resources a person or business can use? Explain your answer.

   _____

   _____

What a Waste

Unless your home is outside of a city and you get your water from a well, then your water traveled through miles of underground pipes before reaching your home. Every drop had to be cleaned first at a water treatment plant. They use filters and chemicals to make sure the water is free of bacteria and other pollution that could make you sick. This process uses electricity, created by burning fossil fuels, as well as other resources. Each drop of water you let flow down the drain unused is a waste of those precious resources.

How many drops are in a gallon of water?

"Who left this faucet on?" Mr. Chambliss asked the students standing by the sink.

"Sorry," Michael apologized, but then he tried to defend himself. "It's practically turned off," he insisted and pointed to the slowly dripping faucet. "There's hardly any water coming out."

Mr. Chambliss thought for a second, and then he called the rest of the class over to the sink.

"If I left this faucet dripping all night," he asked his students, "how much water do you think would be wasted?"

Several students shouted out answers: about a cup, maybe a couple of cups, a quart. The highest guess was one gallon. Mr. Chambliss pointed to a large white bucket sitting on a shelf and asked someone to bring it to him.

"That's an awfully big bucket," Michael said, and a few of the students laughed. The bucket could hold five gallons.

"Maybe," Mr. Chambliss replied, "but let's leave this faucet dripping for a while and see. The drops are falling about once per second. Let's find out how much they add up to in 24 hours."

He put the bucket down into the deep classroom sink, and the drops made a steady, hollow beat as they slowly hit the bottom one by one.

The next day at the same time, Michael headed over to the sink. The bucket was almost full. Marks inside it showed that in just one day, the slow dripping had added up to about four gallons of water.

Mr. Chambliss turned the faucet off to stop the dripping. Then, he hoisted the bucket out of the sink and brought it to the front of the class.

"Our faucet works fine," Mr. Chambliss began, "it just wasn't completely shut off. Imagine that you have a leak because the faucet is broken, and it takes a week to get it fixed. These four gallons would become 28 gallons, and after a month you'd end up with 120 gallons of wasted water. At four gallons a day, times 365 days, you'd have wasted 1,460 gallons a year later. That's enough water to take almost 30 baths!"

Write your answers on the lines below.

1. Give three suggestions for how Mr. Chambliss and his students could use the bucket of water so that it doesn't go to waste.

   _____

   _____

   _____

2. Why is it even more wasteful when a faucet is leaking hot water?

   _____

   _____

3. In 24 hours, the drops added up to 4 gallons of water, so it took 6 hours to get one gallon. The water was dripping at the rate of one drop per second. If one gallon took 6 hours to collect, how many drops are in a gallon?

   _____

4. Think of two things you do that waste water, and then describe how you could change your behavior.

   _____

   _____

Unifying Concepts and Processes

In most places, people pay for the water they use, but they also pay for the water that leaves their homes and flows into the sewer system. Why do people have to pay for the sewage they produce?

_____

_____

What's Next?

Do some research to find out which uses more water, a shower or a bath? What about washing dishes by hand or using a dishwasher? Sometimes the answers to questions like these are surprising.

drawbacks:
disadvantages

marshes: shallow
wetlands that are
home to a variety of
grasses, plants, and
animal life

More than half of U.S.
citizens live within 50
miles of a coast.

In 2005, Hurricane
Katrina was a
frightening reminder
of how powerful
nature can be. Its
damage to the Gulf
Coast made it the
most destructive and
costly natural disaster
in U.S. history. Even
years after the storm,
rebuilding is still
taking place in many
of the hardest-hit
areas.

Rising sea levels can
also be a risk to living
near the water. One
effect of global
warming is that
glaciers and polar ice
caps are melting. It's
happening slowly, but
this warming trend is
causing the level of
the oceans to rise.
According to experts,
the oceans have risen
between six and eight
inches in the last
century.

What are the risks and benefits to living near the ocean?

There's no doubt that living near the ocean has plenty of benefits. Land and houses near the beach are expensive because lots of people want to live there. There's also a limited amount of coastline. Anytime something is in limited supply, especially when it's very desirable, its value rises.

Historically, it made sense that cities were built along coastlines. The first Europeans arrived in America by boat. Fish provided a steady source of food. Later, as trade became important, goods were shipped to and from port cities. People have also always been drawn to the beauty of the ocean. It provides dozens of opportunities for recreation. There are also an abundance of plants and animals for scientists to study.

Coastal living does not come without its fair share of risks and **drawbacks**. Every summer as hurricane season begins, people prepare themselves, their homes, and their businesses for the possibility of a large storm. The high winds and flooding that accompany hurricanes can cause loss of life and enormous damage to property.

Development of coastlines also has a major effect on the local wildlife. As land is cleared to make room for housing and businesses, wildlife is pushed out of its natural habitat. Human development can force animals to live in areas where there is greater competition for food and space. Another result of the growing human populations in coastal areas is that pollution increases. Pollution can upset the delicate balance in a coastal ecosystem and harm both the plants and animals that live there.

Erosion can also become a serious problem. Shorelines naturally erode because of the repeated action of the waves. The effects are even more noticeable, though, when nearby land has been cleared and protective **marshes** have been drained. When human beings change parts of the shoreline landscape, erosion can take place even more quickly. Beaches disappear, more animal habitats are lost, and coastal homes are in danger.

People will always choose to live near the oceans. There are so many things to enjoy about coastal living. As long as human beings make reasonable choices and consider how their actions affect the environment, there's no reason not to enjoy a view of the water.

NAME _____

Circle the letter of the best answer to the question below.

1. Which of the following can cause the loss of animals' habitats in coastal areas?

    a. the high prices of property

    b. erosion

    c. human development

    d. Both b and c

Write your answers on the lines below.

2. What are two reasons why human beings first settled the coasts of America?

_____

_____

3. Why is having a limited amount of coastline a problem?

_____

4. Give three examples of benefits to living close to the ocean.

_____

_____

5. Explain how global warming is linked to rising sea levels.

_____

6. Why has pollution been increasing in coastal areas?

_____

Unifying Concepts and Processes

Think of another example of something in nature that has a limited supply, like the coastline. Is it more valuable for that reason? What will happen when the supply runs out?

_____

_____

_____

The Age of Information

Internet: a worldwide information system of connected computer networks that allow people to communicate and share information

documents: printed or written materials that convey information

online: accessible via a computer or computer network

Internet cafés: also called *cyber cafés*; public places where people can use computers that have Internet access for a small fee

Because more people own computers in the U.S. today, Internet cafés are no longer as popular as they once were. Instead, WiFi cafés have taken their place. People bring their laptop computers to WiFi cafés and can use a wireless high-speed Internet connection.

In 1981, 213 computers were connected to the Internet. In 2007, the number reached 747 million.

In 2007, the United States had the most Internet users, followed by China and Japan. India and Russia had the largest increases in users.

How has the Internet changed society?

A remarkable invention changed the world in the early 1990s. It changed the way people worked, studied, communicated, and conducted research. The **Internet** made information available in a whole new way.

Starting in the mid-1970s, researchers began designing the Internet, a system that allows people to send and receive electronic **documents** and files, better known as e-mail. Tim Berners-Lee had the idea to create pages of text and images that could be shared on the Internet. He called it the *World Wide Web*. In 1991, he put the Web on the Internet. Suddenly, people all over the world were linked together.

Speed and access are two of the most important elements of the Internet. People can send and receive documents in seconds. Not only can information move quickly, almost anyone can access it. Before the invention of the printing press, only the wealthiest members of society had access to books. As books became more common and less expensive, they reached a wider audience. Public libraries made more information available to a greater number of people than ever before.

With the invention of the Internet, millions of people gained access to enormous amounts of information—more than could be held in thousands of libraries. Now, a child in Brazil has access to the same **online** information as a professor in France, a dad in India, and a biologist in Africa do. While not everyone owns a computer, Internet access can be found in libraries, schools, and **Internet cafés** around the world.

The Internet is especially important in the world of science, where new discoveries are made every day. Sharing one's results is a basic principle of being a scientist. The work of a single scientist is based on hundreds of discoveries that came before. Without building on the knowledge of others, progress in the scientific world would nearly come to a standstill. Think of the airplane, the radio, antibiotics, and the electric light bulb. They were all the result of scientists building on each other's knowledge.

Today, scientists can conduct research online and have access to the most up-to-date information available. They can learn about the progress that their colleagues all over the world have made. They can even work with someone thousands of miles away to solve a problem.

Underline the correct answer from the two choices you are given.

1. There are more Internet users in (China, the United States) than any other country.

2. Today, the rates of Internet use around the world are (growing, remaining steady).

3. The Internet makes information more available to (wealthy people, nearly everyone).

4. If you visit (a WiFi café, an Internet café) you do not need to bring a computer with you.

Write your answers on the lines below.

5. How were the first public libraries similar to the invention of the Internet?

_____

_____

6. In your own words, explain why the invention of the Internet is so important to the world of science.

_____

_____

7. Why do scientists need to share knowledge with one another?

_____

_____

8. How does the Internet provide educational opportunities for different people all over the world?

_____

_____

_____

9. Dr. Rahman has been studying the way that a certain strain of the flu virus is transmitted. He has a breakthrough and publishes his results in an online scientific journal. Explain how the impact on the scientific world might be different if Dr. Rahman had had his breakthrough before the Internet became widely used.

_____

_____

Healthy Computer Habits

repetitive strain injury: an injury caused by a repeated activity

carpal tunnel syndrome: pain and weakness from a squeezed nerve inside the wrist

tendons: body tissue that connects the muscles

Computer use is not the only cause of carpal tunnel syndrome. Working at a machine in a factory, laying bricks, knitting, and even playing musical instruments can also cause it.

How can computer use hurt you?

Computers have changed our lives. They can also affect our bodies. Too much time at the computer can lead to repetitive strain injuries and sore eyes.

A **repetitive strain injury** can happen when someone does the same movement over and over again. For computer users, **carpal tunnel syndrome** is quite common. The carpal tunnel is a narrow tunnel of bones and muscle in the wrist. Inside this tunnel are nine **tendons** and a major nerve that powers your hand. Inflamed tendons or even just frequently working with a bent wrist can squeeze the nerve. This leads to pain, numbness, and weakness in the arm and wrist—all symptoms of carpal tunnel syndrome.

You can avoid this problem by sitting correctly. Sit straight up, with your head and hips in a straight line. Your shoulders should be low and relaxed, not hunched over, because tension can be another cause of carpal tunnel syndrome. Your elbows should be at a right angle. Most importantly, your wrists should be in a straight line from your knuckles to your elbow. Let your wrists float above the mouse or keyboard; don't lean them on the mouse pad or desk.

Have you ever had sore eyes or headaches after using the computer for a long time? Computers can cause eye strain because the screens are made up of tiny dots called *pixels*, which your eyes are constantly trying to focus on. In addition, people don't blink as often when they are using the computer, so their eyes dry out. You can reduce glare on the screen by making sure that any lights are positioned at the sides of the computer, not behind or above you. Dusting the screen regularly, sitting about two feet away from it, and trying to blink often can help you avoid eye problems and headaches.

Taking breaks is also important. It's good to take a 15-minute break from any kind of work every two hours. However, people are learning that "micro-breaks," like a 30-second break every 10 minutes, are also good for computer users. Take half a minute to stretch your fingers, let your hands relax and hang limp from your sides, or focus on a distant object to give your eyes a change. Take a longer break to get a drink or walk around the block. A little exercise will give your body more oxygen and more energy. Taking breaks can actually help you to do more in the long run.

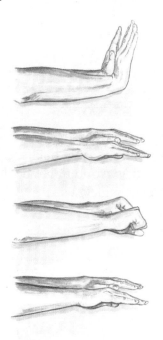

Circle the letter of the best answer to the question below.

1. Which of the following will not help you avoid eyestrain at the computer?

   a. keeping the screen dusted

   b. sitting about two feet away

   c. positioning a light behind you when you are at the computer

   d. taking micro-breaks

Write your answers on the lines below.

2. What are the symptoms of carpal tunnel syndrome?

   _____

3. According to the selection, what do computer users have in common with people who knit, lay bricks, or play an instrument that can lead to carpal tunnel syndrome?

   _____

4. Kyle likes to work at his dad's computer. The chair is hard to adjust, so he usually just leaves it where it is. This means that his arms have to rest on the keyboard tray. Why is this a bad idea?

   _____

   _____

5. Why is taking breaks when you are working on the computer important?

   _____

6. Why can computer users develop eye strain and headaches?

   _____

7. Many researchers have linked an increase in computer use to an increase in obesity, or the number of people who are overweight. Why do you think there is a link between the two? What can people do to make sure their computer use doesn't affect their weight?

   _____

   _____

   _____

New Technologies = New Careers

industry: businesses that provide a particular product or service

occupations: jobs or professions

class: a particular group in society

diplomats: people whose job it is to keep peaceful relations between different countries

professional class: group of workers in society who are college-educated and make an above-average salary

In less than 150 years, the number of people involved in farming has changed dramatically in the United States. In 1870, nearly half the American population worked in agriculture. By 2006, this number had dropped to less than one percent of the population.

Does the industry you'll work in as an adult even exist today?

Fifty years ago, the only people working with computers were a handful of scientists and engineers. Today, the computer **industry** employees millions of people, such as computer programmers, Web site developers, and computer repair people. Computer technology brought with it an entire range of new careers, but it wasn't the first invention to do this.

Throughout history, important discoveries and inventions changed the way people live and work. In fact, human civilization began with the technological breakthrough of agriculture. People no longer had to spend all of their time hunting and gathering food. This change brought about new skills and even new **occupations**. For example, someone needed to guard the stored crops from thieves and wild animals.

People who weren't involved in the growing or handling of crops could spend their time perfecting other skills. Crafts such as metalworking, pottery, and weaving gave rise to a new **class** of craftspeople. As work became more specialized, people began trading with each other to get things they didn't have the time or knowledge to make themselves. Traders traveled the world transporting goods from where they were made to where they were needed.

As traders went farther and farther from home, there was a need for better transportation technologies. Shipbuilding, sailing, mapmaking, and exploring became sources of income for many people across the globe. Soldiers and **diplomats** were needed to ensure that traders traveled safely.

In the late 1700s, the Industrial Revolution caused the biggest change in civilization since the birth of agriculture. Steam engines powered all sorts of new machines, and factories sprang up across Europe. People flocked to the cities to work in the factories, or to service the machines used there.

Many craftspeople suddenly found themselves out of work. Machine-made goods were much cheaper to produce than hand-made ones. Many of these people began working in factories, but the growing populations of the cities meant that other occupations were in demand as well. A **professional class** emerged that included doctors, lawyers, and teachers.

During the twentieth century, the internal combustion engine was the invention that created millions of new jobs. The automobile, airline, and oil industries are still huge employers today. What new technology will change the way we work in the 21st century?

Write your answers on the lines below.

1. Briefly describe why the invention of agriculture created so many other occupations.

_____

_____

2. A woman makes her living delivering pizzas. Name three inventions or technologies that had to exist before her job became possible.

_____   _____   _____

3. List two jobs that didn't exist before automobiles were invented.

_____   _____

4. List one job that would no longer exist if a device was invented that could instantly clean water, no matter how dirty it was.

_____

5. What effect do you think the invention of the tractor had on the number of people employed in agriculture? Explain your answer.

_____

_____

6. As fossil fuels become scarcer and more expensive, how do you think each occupation listed below will be affected?

Gas station owner: _____

Farmer: _____

Windmill manufacturer: _____

Scientist working in optics, or the study of light: _____

Construction worker: _____

What's Next?

Choose one of the following technologies and do some research to see how it may change the future: the use of hydrogen as a power source, nanotechnology, biofuels, genetic engineering, or virtual reality.

Review

Circle the letter of the best answer to each question below.

1. What does a calorie measure?

   a. the amount of carbohydrates in food

   b. the potential energy in food

   c. the number of fat grams a food contains

   d. the RDA for a food

2. Which of the following is not a reason that people have limited access to clean water?

   a. droughts

   b. poverty

   c. working sewage systems

   d. global warming

3. The Internet was first introduced in the

   a. 1950s.

   b. 1960s.

   c. 1970s.

   d. 1980s.

Write **true** or **false** next to each statement below.

4. _____ Level of activity is the only important factor to consider when calculating the number of calories you should eat each day.

5. _____ Vitamin D is the only vitamin your body makes.

6. _____ Buildings that have some flexibility are the most likely to collapse during an earthquake.

7. _____ Most of the water on Earth's surface is salt water.

8. _____ In the United States, fossil fuels are burned to create clean, drinkable water.

9. _____ The destruction of marshlands has no effect on the erosion of coastal areas.

10. _____ Since the invention of the Internet, more information is available to larger numbers of people than ever before.

Write your answers on the lines below.

11. What are empty calories?

_____

12. Why is eating a balanced diet important?

_____

13. Why do you need to eat foods that contain water-soluble vitamins every day?

_____

14. What is one way in which engineers identify how strong or weak a building might be during an earthquake?

_____

15. Give one example of a way that engineers have found to make buildings earthquake resistant.

_____

16. Even though water covers two-thirds of Earth's surface, why do many people not have enough drinkable water?

_____

17. Why is it important to fix a leaky faucet as soon as possible?

_____

18. How does human development along the coastlines affect wildlife?

_____

19. How is the impact that the Internet had on science similar to the impact the invention of the printing press had?

_____

20. Describe the proper way to sit and type at the computer.

_____

21. Name one technology and a career that didn't exist before the computer's invention.

_____

Lesson 7.1 — Positively Radioactive

electromagnetic spectrum: the entire range of electromagnetic waves, including everything from giant radio waves to tiny gamma rays

beneficial: creating good health or good results

radioactive decay: the process of an unstable atom losing energy and particles as it becomes stable

sterilize: kill or remove germs, bacteria, or other microscopic organisms

tumors: abnormal masses of tissue in the body that don't have any useful function

Radio waves, microwaves, and the UHF and VHF waves that carry television signals all have longer wavelengths than visible light. These waves are part of the electromagnetic spectrum, so they are forms of radiation, but they don't contain enough energy to be dangerous to human beings.

Is all radiation harmful?

The **electromagnetic spectrum** contains all wavelengths of radiation. Some of this energy is harmless, like visible light, but some of it can be dangerous. When people other than scientists use the word *radiation*, they are usually referring to the dangerous wavelengths of energy—wavelengths that are shorter than visible light. These include ultraviolet light, X-rays, and gamma rays. Organisms exposed to high enough levels of radiation can be burned, become sick, or even die.

Radiation can also be **beneficial**, though, if it's used carefully. Here are just a few of the ways that human beings use radiation.

- Isotopes undergo **radioactive decay** at a very steady rate called a *half-life*. The approximate age of a substance containing isotopes can be found by measuring how much of the isotope has already decayed and changed into a different element.

- Radiation in high enough doses will kill any living organism. Radiation can be used to **sterilize** medical equipment. Radiation can also be used on medical waste to kill any germs or other disease-causing organisms before it's sent to a landfill. Even food is sometimes treated with radiation to kill bacteria, insects, or mold that might damage it.

- X-rays pass right through the soft tissues in the body, but denser parts, especially bones, will block them. A photographic plate creates an image by absorbing the X-rays that pass through the body. The X-ray image is like a shadow cast by the insides of a body.

- When cancers are untreatable by other methods, radiation can be used to control the growth of **tumors**. Cancer cells are unhealthy cells that reproduce at a dangerous rate and create tumors that can interfere with the body's normal functions. Radiation kills cancer cells by damaging their DNA. Unfortunately, radiation often damages good cells as well.

- Probably the most common use of radiation in everyday life is inside smoke detectors. A smoke detector contains an extremely small amount of the isotope americium-241 between two metal plates. An electrical current flows from one plate, through the isotope, and into the other plate. If a whiff of smoke enters the detector, the electrical current is interrupted, and the alarm goes off.

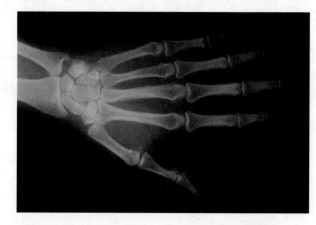

Circle the letter of the best answer to each question below.

1. X-rays _____ the body in order to create an image of what's going on inside it.

   a. reflect off

   b. illuminate

   c. travel through

   d. heat

2. Smoke detectors contain _____ of the element *americium*.

   a. molecules

   b. ions

   c. gamma rays

   d. isotopes

3. Which of the following is not released during radioactive decay?

   a. alpha particles

   b. gamma rays

   c. beta particles

   d. microwaves

Write your answer on the lines below.

4. Explain why radiation can be both helpful and harmful when used to treat cancer.

   _____

   _____

Unifying Concepts and Processes

The harmful effects of radiation are sometimes not seen in the organisms that were poisoned but appear in the next generation instead. Their offspring then suffer from a variety of different defects. Explain why.

_____

_____

Naming the Stars

celestial: relating to the sky

mythology: all of the stories or legends of a group of people, such as the Greeks or Romans

Most galaxies have catalog numbers, but our galaxy is one exception. The ancient Greek astronomers thought it looked like a river of milk, so Earth's galaxy was named the *Milky Way*.

Naming comets after their discoverers is common today. The first comet to be named after a person was Halley's Comet. Edmond Halley didn't discover it, but he was the first to realize that it can be seen from Earth every 76 years. The scientific name for a comet includes the year it was discovered and a letter that tells the order of its discovery.

What are constellations, and how are they named?

Jupiter, Draco, and the Milky Way are all **celestial** bodies, or objects that reside in the sky. Astronomy is the scientific study of the stars, planets, moons, and other celestial bodies. As new objects are discovered, astronomers in the International Astronomical Union (IAU) assign them names.

Astronomy is an old science that dates back to the earliest days of human history. Many astronomical names that we still use today come from Greek and Roman **mythology**, including the names of the planets. Earth is the only planet that does not have a mythological name. The word *earth* is an Old English word that means "ground."

Some of the most interesting astronomical names are those of constellations, or groups of stars. Early astronomers looked at the night skies and connected groups of stars to form outlines in various shapes. They saw animals, like Aries the Ram, Cygnus the Swan, and Draco the Dragon. They named images of people after mythological figures, like Hercules and Orion. They also named constellations after objects, like Libra the Balance and Corona the Crown.

Because astronomers today have access to such powerful telescopes, millions of individual stars can be seen. The brightest stars in the night sky— the ones that can be seen without the use of high-tech telescopes—are the only ones that have proper names. Most of these names are Arabic because Middle Eastern astronomers discovered and mapped them hundreds of years ago. The millions of stars that have been discovered more recently have been given catalog numbers by the IAU based on their locations.

Have you ever wished you could name a star? Some private companies allow people to purchase the rights to naming a star. The star is then listed by that name in the company's registry. These names are not recognized by the IAU or the scientific community, but it can still be fun to think that you named a star that lies light years away from Earth.

Halley's Comet

Write **true** or **false** next to each statement below.

1. _____ Unlike the Milky Way Galaxy, most galaxies are given numbers rather than names.

2. _____ Halley's Comet can be seen 76 days out of every year.

3. _____ It is possible for regular citizens to name stars, but those names aren't recognized by the IAU.

4. _____ The names of most of the planets are Arabic words.

5. _____ Constellations are individual stars that can be connected to form shapes.

Write your answers on the lines below.

6. What is a celestial body? Give two examples.

   _____

   _____

7. How did the Greeks and Romans name celestial bodies?

   _____

   _____

8. Who names most new celestial bodies today?

   _____

9. How are comets named? What information does the common name give you, compared to the scientific name?

   _____

   _____

10. How were the constellations named?

   _____

   _____

Searching for a Signal

paradox: a statement that seems like it should be true but isn't, or a statement that seems like it should be false but is actually true

extra-terrestrial: beyond Earth

signals: any kinds of messages, sounds, or effects used to communicate

When the scientists at NASA launched the *Pioneer 10* and *Pioneer 11* spacecraft in the early 1970s, they attached identical plaques to both vehicles. These plaques contained symbols showing where our sun is located in relation to other nearby stars, a simple map of our solar system, and drawings of a man and woman.

A few years later, *Voyager 1* and *2* carried special gold phonograph records into space. They contained words spoken in 55 languages, a message from President Jimmy Carter, and samples of many different styles of music.

What would a message from outer space look or sound like?

Astronomers estimate that the universe contains about 70 sextillion stars—a 7 followed by 22 zeroes. It's hard to imagine such a huge number, but if you counted the individual grains of sand on every beach on Earth, you would be somewhere close. The vast size of the universe leads most scientists to believe that life forms must exist beyond our planet. Is any of that life intelligent?

In 1950, the physicist Enrico Fermi famously asked, "Where are they?" He argued that the universe is extremely old and large, so it seems obvious that other advanced civilizations must have developed in places other than Earth. It's odd, then, that no evidence of them has ever been found. This idea became known as *Fermi's* **Paradox**.

A serious search began about ten years later to locate the missing evidence. One of the most basic signs of intelligence is the ability to communicate, and one of the simplest ways to communicate across long distances is to use radio waves. The scientists in a program called *SETI*, the Search for **Extra-Terrestrial** Intelligence, began scanning the skies for unusual radio **signals**.

Random static fills the universe because objects in space are naturally emitting waves of energy all the time. Scientists in the SETI program carefully search among the radio frequencies for anything that sounds like a signal. The universe is so vast, though, that this job is like searching for one green grain of sand hidden among trillions of brown ones.

After more than 40 years of searching, SETI has yet to find any pattern or signal that can't be explained as coming from a natural source. One problem may be that the search is limited to radio waves. The spectrum also contains light waves, microwaves, gamma rays, and other wavelengths beyond radio frequencies. Recently, SETI scientists have broadened their search to include the use of microwaves and visible light to detect signals.

SETI may never locate the evidence it hopes to find. Some scientists think the Rare Earth hypothesis is more likely to be true. The Rare Earth hypothesis states that Earth is an extremely unusual planet, and intelligent life arose here only because of a long series of unlikely occurrences. We are only just beginning to discover planets outside of our solar system, though. Whether Earth is a common or uncommon planet is yet to be proven.

NAME _____

Circle the letter of the best answer to the question below.

1. Which of the following is a sign of intelligent life?

    a. the ability to fly

    b. the ability to use signs and symbols

    c. the ability to hunt

    d. All of the above

Write your answers on the lines below.

2. What does SETI stand for?

    _____

3. Explain the Fermi Paradox.

    _____

    _____

4. What does the Rare Earth hypothesis say about intelligent life in the universe?

    _____

    _____

5. Even if we have no idea what the message says, an unnatural pattern in a radio wave would indicate intelligent life. Why?

    _____

    _____

6. Some people think that the SETI program is a waste of time and money. What do you think? Explain your answer.

    _____

    _____

What's Next?

SETI has a program that you can download onto your computer that lets them use a small part of your hard drive. The program, called *SETI@home*, connects computers from across the world to create one giant supercomputer that can be used for their research. Be sure to ask your parents before you download this program.

Spectrum Science
Grade 6

Chapter 7 Lesson 3

133

Flying Through Time

gliders: aircraft that glide through the air without engines

dirigible: an aircraft that is lighter than air, can be steered, and has a means of being propelled

supersonic: moving at or faster than the speed of sound (761 miles per hour at sea level)

Planes were first used in warfare during World War I. Early in the war, planes were used for spying and gathering information. It wasn't long before the pilots become involved in the fighting. By the time WWII began, planes were an important wartime tool, and greater numbers were produced specifically for the war.

In 1927, Charles Lindbergh accomplished the first solo flight across the Atlantic, from New York to Paris.

After the terrorist attacks on 9/11, all U.S. flights were cancelled. It was the first time in almost a century that there were no commercial planes in American skies.

What path did human beings take in learning how to fly?

400 B.C.—The Chinese invented kites. Human beings began to think seriously of ways they could take to the skies.

1485—Leonardo da Vinci was an artist and a talented inventor. He studied the flight of birds and created many designs that illustrated ways people might fly. One design became the basis for modern helicopters.

1783—The French Montgolfier Brothers launched the first hot air balloon.

1799—George Cayley designed a variety of **gliders**, some of which were tested by human beings. He spent 50 years perfecting and improving his designs. He also came up with the first designs for the modern airplane.

1852—Henri Giffard invented the first steam-engine **dirigible**, or airship.

1891—Otto Lilienthal studied the flight of birds and tried to incorporate some of his observations into the designs for his gliders. The Wright Brothers used his book on flight when they designed the first plane.

1903—The Wright Brothers learned everything they could about earlier attempts at flight. They added an engine to a glider, and after many failed attempts, the first plane took to the air. The flight lasted 12 seconds.

1924—The first successful helicopter was invented by Étienne Oehmichen. An unsuccessful earlier version of a helicopter was invented in 1907.

1947—Chuck Yeager broke the sound barrier in a **supersonic** aircraft, the *Bell X-1*, which was powered by rockets. He flew at 662 miles per hour.

1961—Russian Yuri Gagarin, traveling in the spacecraft *Vostok 1*, was the first human being to orbit Earth.

1969—Neil Armstrong walked on the moon during the first manned mission to the moon on the *Apollo* spacecraft.

1970—The flight of the first jumbo jet, the Boeing 747, took place. It could carry more passengers than any other aircraft—an honor it held for 35 years.

1976—British Airways was the first to offer commercial trips across the Atlantic in a supersonic jet, the Concorde.

1981—NASA launched its first space shuttle, *Columbia*. During the shuttle's two-day voyage, it orbited Earth 36 times.

2001—Dennis Tito, the first space tourist, paid millions of dollars for the chance to journey to the International Space Station.

Read each pair of items below. Place a check mark next to the event that occurred first in each pair.

1. _____ Human beings orbited Earth.   _____ NASA launched its first space shuttle.

2. _____ The first Concorde flight took place. _____ The first jumbo jet flight took place.

3. _____ The first gliders were invented.   _____ Kites were invented.

4. _____ Planes were used in wartime.   _____ *Apollo* journeyed to the moon.

Write your answers on the lines below.

5. What element of nature did human beings study as they tried to learn the secrets of flight?

_____

6. What made World War I different from earlier wars in history?

_____

7. Choose one form of air transportation and explain how it relied on the invention of an earlier form.

_____

_____

8. Based on the information in the time line, what kind of progress do you think will take place in the future of flight?

_____

_____

Unifying Concepts and Processes

Compare the time line entry for the launch of the first space shuttle with some of the earlier entries, like the first gliders or the Wright Brothers' plane. Why do you think some of the earlier forms of flight had one or two inventors, while no one is credited with the flight of the first space shuttle?

_____

_____

The Interesting Life of Henry Cavendish

contraption: a device or gadget

Cavendish's machine was so sensitive that even the movement of air in a room could interfere with his measurements. To solve this problem, he set up the machine in a sealed room, and then peered inside through a small hole in the wall, using a telescope to get his measurements.

Why were many of Henry Cavendish's discoveries unknown until long after his death?

Mad scientists are popular figures in films and on TV. With wild hair and crazy grins, they spend all their time in labs, surrounded by bubbling beakers and brightly-colored test tubes. In reality, however, scientists are hard-working professionals doing their jobs like workers in any other field. That's not to say science that history doesn't have its share of interesting people, though. Henry Cavendish was certainly one of them.

Born in 1731, Cavendish was one of the most brilliant scientists of his time, but his incredible shyness led to some odd behaviors. He came from an extremely wealthy family that was part of British royalty, which meant that Cavendish didn't have to go out into the world to work. Instead, he isolated himself inside his home and spent his life conducting scientific research in a large laboratory.

Cavendish did attend weekly meetings with other scientists where they discussed their research. These scientists recognized Cavendish's talents, but they also understood how fearful he was of other people. When guests came to the meetings, they were asked not to speak directly to Cavendish or he would become uncomfortable and walk away. They suggested that standing somewhere near him and then talking to no one in particular was a better approach. If Cavendish had something to say, he would speak up.

Despite his incredible shyness, Cavendish was an accomplished researcher. He made amazing discoveries about electricity, the elements, the nature of gases, and the conservation of energy. Unfortunately, Cavendish was very secretive about his work. No one knew the true extent of his genius until decades after his death. The physicist James Clerk Maxwell went through his papers in the late 1800s and saw that many other scientists had received credit for important discoveries that Cavendish had accomplished years earlier but had never published.

In the 1790s, Cavendish inherited a complicated **contraption** from another scientist. He studied the gravitational pull of large weights hanging from the machine against other, smaller weights. Cavendish used his calculations from this machine to determine Earth's weight to be six billion trillion metric tons. Amazingly, he was just one percent off from the weight known today.

Circle the letter of the best answer to each question below.

1. Cavendish's machine helped him calculate

   a. the force of Earth's gravity.

   b. Earth's circumference.

   c. Earth's weight.

   d. All of the above

2. Cavendish's machine used

   a. the force of gravity.

   b. weights.

   c. electricity.

   d. Both a and b

Write your answers on the lines below.

3. How do you think Cavendish's shyness helped him in his scientific work?

   _____

   _____

   _____

4. How did Cavendish's shyness interfere with his ability to be a good scientist?

   _____

   _____

   _____

What's Next?

In the 20th century, Albert Einstein became the stereotype of the eccentric scientist. His hair was part of it, but he also introduced ideas about space and time that were difficult for many people to understand. Was he really eccentric, though? Read more about Einstein's life and discover why so many other scientists consider him to be the greatest scientific mind of all time.

The Wizard of Horticulture

horticulturist: a person who breeds, raises, and studies plants

cultivated: raised, developed, or tended to

patent: a license that gives one right of ownership to an invention

crossbreeding: breeding two different types of plants with one another

grafted: inserted a twig or bud of a plant into the stem of another plant so that they grow together

"The scientist is a lover of truth for the very love of truth itself, wherever it may lead."
—Luther Burbank, horticulturist and botanist

On some of Burbank's notecards, he made actual prints of his fruit. He cut the fruit in half and pressed it onto a notecard. The fruit juice left a stain on the card, and Burbank recorded his notes about the fruit beside its impression.

Have you ever heard of a plucot? The plum-apricot combination was one of Burbank's creations.

How does a person invent a plant?

You might not have heard of **horticulturist** Luther Burbank, but you're probably familiar with some of his inventions. As a matter of fact, if you've eaten fast food French fries, there's a good chance they were made with the Russet Burbank potato. Are you surprised to hear something like a potato called an invention? After all, potatoes are natural, not something human beings created, right? Yes and no. Potatoes do grow naturally, of course. However, when a fruit or vegetable has been bred to have certain characteristics, it can sometimes be considered an invention.

This is a relatively recent development. During Luther Burbank's life, he **cultivated** more than 800 varieties of plants. The U.S. government did not yet allow inventors to **patent** plants. It wasn't until the patent laws changed after his death that Burbank was awarded patents on many of his creations.

Burbank first grew interested in plants during the time he spent in his mother's garden as a child. When he bought a small farm for himself, he quickly developed the Burbank potato. He sold the rights to the potato and moved to California in 1875. In his Santa Rosa greenhouse and in the fields on his property, Burbank began experimenting by **crossbreeding** plants that had desirable characteristics. Then, he **grafted** the seedlings onto the parent plants. This allowed him to get quick results. He could choose the best plants in each batch and breed them.

One of Burbank's goals was to create crops that were resistant to disease. He wanted foods to taste better and last longer, too. Even though many of his experiments involved edible plants, Burbank also worked with trees and flowers. In fact, one of his best known inventions was the Shasta daisy. He also experimented with roses and different varieties of cacti.

Burbank was not considered a serious scientist by many other scientists of the time. They believed that his methods and data collection weren't very scientific and that he was too focused on getting results. Others disagreed. Burbank grew thousands of plants at a time. His records had to be organized in order for him to keep track of so many plants. In addition to taking detailed notes about his results, Burbank used photography as a scientific tool. He had a studio on his farm and used the pictures to keep track of different varieties of plants, as well as to compare strains of a plant or fruit.

Use the words in the box to complete the sentences below.

bred	cultivate	patent	horticulturist

1. A person who has invented something new might apply for a _____ with the U.S. government.

2. A _____ is similar to a botanist, a scientist who studies the biology of plant life.

3. For his entire career, Burbank _____ plants to have specific characteristics.

4. To _____ a plant is to raise and tend to it.

Write your answers on the lines below.

5. When is a plant considered a human invention?

_____

_____

6. Why didn't some scientists take Burbank's work very seriously?

_____

_____

7. Why does the author of the selection say that Burbank used photography as a scientific tool?

_____

_____

8. Name four plants that Burbank cultivated.

_____ _____ _____ _____

9. Give two examples of characteristics that Burbank tried to incorporate into his plants.

_____

_____

The Science of Ancient China

shadow clock: a timekeeping device that used shadows created by sunlight to mark time; a sundial is an advanced version of a shadow clock

abacus: a frame with beads that slide on metal rods that is used to make mathematical calculations

precision: the act of being accurate or precise

papyrus: strips of the papyrus plant that have been woven together to form a writing surface

The history of human flight also begins in China with the invention of kites 3,000 years ago. The kites carried messages, sent signals, and measured distances.

What inventions did ancient Chinese scientists make?

Around 1300, the Italian traveler Marco Polo published a book about his travels through Asia. The book was a huge success across Europe, but many readers doubted the truthfulness of Polo's stories. His descriptions of Chinese culture and technology seemed like science fiction to them. The tales were true, though. For 2,000 years, China was the most scientifically advanced civilization on Earth. Chinese inventions and discoveries played a major role in creating our modern world.

Inventions, such as the **shadow clock** and the **abacus**, helped ancient Chinese astronomers make some of the earliest discoveries about our universe. For example, the first solar eclipse was recorded in China more than 4,000 years ago. The **precision** of Chinese timekeeping was particularly helpful for tracking comets. *The Book of Silk*, written in 400 B.C., lists 29 comets that crossed the skies during the previous 300 years.

As in Europe, Chinese alchemists were trying to find ways to change ordinary metal into gold. They were also searching for chemicals that would let them live forever. These experiments led them to discover a mixture that produced an explosive black powder. It was soon being used to create fireworks and weapons. By Marco Polo's day, this powder, today known as *gunpowder*, had spread from China, across the Middle East, and into Europe.

Chinese scholars first wrote about magnetism more than 2,000 years ago, but it took a few centuries before this force was used for navigation. The first true compass appeared in China about 1,000 years ago. A magnetized needle hung from a silk thread inside a box with markings that showed directions. Chinese sailors used compasses whenever it was too dark or cloudy to navigate by the stars or the sun.

Paper was invented in China about 2,000 years ago, but Chinese rulers tried to keep it a secret from the rest of the world. Other cultures had been writing on animal skins or **papyrus**, but papermaking technology eventually spread outside of China by the 1400s.

Paper was flexible, thin, and inexpensive. It was the perfect material to use for printing books. By the late 1400s, Johannes Gutenberg's printing presses were up and running throughout Europe. They allowed scientific knowledge, including Chinese discoveries and technologies, to spread rapidly through Europe and kick off the Renaissance.

NAME _____

Circle the letter of the best answer to each question below.

1. Which of the following was not invented in ancient China?

   a. the compass

   b. gunpowder

   c. papyrus

   d. kites

2. Many Europeans thought Marco Polo's stories about China were untrue because

   a. he described human flight and space travel.

   b. Polo was known for telling lies.

   c. Chinese technology was far more advanced than European technology of the time.

   d. he never actually went to China.

Write your answers on the lines below.

3. Why did ancient Chinese sailors use compasses only when it was cloudy or dark?

   _____

   _____

4. What did Chinese alchemists have in common with European alchemists?

   _____

   _____

5. Explain how Chinese culture helped fuel the European Renaissance.

   _____

   _____

Unifying Concepts and Processes

Why do you think precise timekeeping is an important part of astronomy?

_____

_____

Discovering the West

expedition: a long journey made for a purpose, such as exploration

document: to make a record by writing, drawing, and/or photographing

zoology: the study of animals

Many of the animals that were first recorded by the expedition are common to us today. They include grizzly bears, prairie dogs, pronghorn antelopes, white-tailed deer, and mountain goats.

According to Lewis and Clark's journals, many of the animals they encountered, even grizzly bears and wolves, seemed tame. Native Americans rarely hunted these animals, so they had no fear of human predators.

Sacagawea was a Shoshone woman who helped the men survive the first harsh winter of their journey. Sacagawea helped the explorers communicate with many of the native people they encountered.

What were the purposes of the Lewis and Clark expedition?

In 1803, President Thomas Jefferson signed a treaty with France that made the Louisiana Purchase official. Overnight, the young United States nearly doubled in size. The following year, Jefferson initiated an **expedition** into the new territory. Native Americans had been living there for thousands of years, but Europeans knew little about this western land.

Meriwether Lewis and William Clark led a group of more than 30 men on a journey to explore this mysterious new world. No one knew what to expect, so they prepared for a long, hard journey by bringing plenty of supplies, including journals and pens.

Their main mission was to establish relationships with Indian nations of the West and to search for a water route to the Pacific Ocean. However, President Jefferson was a man of science. He thirsted for knowledge of the natural world. He wanted Lewis and Clark to make detailed observations of the plants and wildlife they encountered in the West. They were to collect samples and **document** whatever they discovered.

During their exploration, Lewis spent much of his time on land, observing animals, plants, and rocks. Although he had spent most of his life as an army captain, Lewis studied botany and geology to prepare for the trip. He even included scientific reference books in the expedition's supplies.

The group journeyed up the Missouri River, across the Rocky Mountains, and on toward the Pacific Northwest. The explorers took careful notes about what they discovered as they traveled.

On their expedition, Lewis and Clark observed and described 120 new mammals, birds, reptiles, and fish, as well as 172 plant species. They collected many samples for future study and occasionally shipped samples back East, including a live prairie dog!

Lewis and Clark's successful expedition lasted for two years, four months, and ten days. They established bonds with Native American nations and discovered routes to the West. Their contributions to science, though, especially in the areas of **zoology** and botany, were every bit as important.

Once the boundaries between East and West had been crossed, more and more people attempted the journey. Lewis and Clark didn't just give Americans a peek through a window to the West; they opened the door.

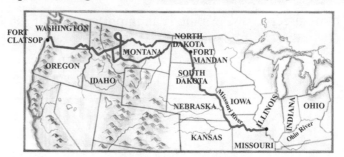

Circle the letter of the best answer to the question below.

1. Why does the author call Thomas Jefferson a "man of science"?

   a. Jefferson was a botanist.

   b. Jefferson was curious about the natural world.

   c. Jefferson taught science to Lewis and Clark.

   d. All of the above

Write your answers on the lines below.

2. Why was it important for Lewis and Clark to keep journals?

   _____

3. What types of scientific investigating did Lewis and Clark perform?

   _____

4. How did Lewis and Clark's journey help zoology?

   _____

5. Geology is the study of Earth's structure. How do you think Lewis and Clark's discoveries about geology in the West helped people who traveled there later?

   _____

   _____

6. Today, wild animals in the West tend to avoid human beings, but Lewis and Clark wrote that animals mostly had no fear of them. What do you think caused this change?

   _____

   _____

Unifying Concepts and Processes

Many exploration teams of new lands have included scientists. In the 1830s, the main goal of the English ship called the *HMS Beagle* was to map South America. Charles Darwin came along to observe the wildlife and plants they encountered. European explorations of the New World often carried along scientists. How did this practice help the world of science?

_____

_____

For the Love of Chimps

tools: devices used to make work easier

vegetarians: those who eat only plant materials and no meat

primatologist: a scientist who studies the behavior of primates, like apes and monkeys

field study: a study of animals in their natural habitat

"Every single day, we make an impact on the world. . . . And we all have a choice as to what sort of impact we're going to make each day."
—Jane Goodall, **primatologist**

Goodall's time at Gombe turned into the longest **field study** of animals in their natural habitat.

It is common to give research subjects numbers to identify them. Instead, Goodall used names, like Fifi, Flo, David Greybeard, and Mr. McGregor. To some scientists, this seemed unprofessional because scientists usually distance themselves from their subjects. Goodall believed that the animals she studied had personalities and emotions, so naming them made sense.

How did Jane Goodall contribute to scientific knowledge of chimpanzees?

Jane Goodall loved animals ever since she was a small child. When she was in her mid-20s, she began working in Africa with the well-known paleontologists, the Leakeys. Louis Leakey suggested that Goodall study the chimpanzees at the Gombe Stream Chimpanzee Reserve. Goodall had no idea that she would become so interested and involved that she would continue her observations for the next 40 years.

Goodall had to be very patient at first. She spent hour after hour in silent observation, using her binoculars from a distance. It took several months for the chimps to become used to her presence. One of Goodall's first important observations was that chimpanzees could make and use **tools**. She noticed chimps using blades of grass and twigs to fish termites out of their nests. Goodall's discovery forced scientists to rethink how they defined human beings. Until that point, scientists thought that only human beings used tools, which set them apart from animals.

Goodall also made several other discoveries about chimpanzee behavior that changed what scientists thought they knew about them. Chimps were believed to be **vegetarians**, but Goodall saw them kill and eat other animals, such as wild pigs. Chimps were also thought to live peacefully with one another, but Goodall's observations painted a different picture. She saw that different groups of chimpanzees sometimes fought. She even observed a four-year war take place. This was the first time that a long-term war had been observed in any group other than human beings.

In spite of some violent behaviors, Goodall also witnessed many tender moments. For example, she saw a teenage male chimp "adopt" a young chimp that had been orphaned, even though they weren't related. She also observed many loving family relationships—between mates, parents and children, and siblings. Over and over, Goodall was struck by behaviors that she saw as being similar to the way human family groups interact.

In 1977, Goodall founded the Jane Goodall Institute. The goal of the institute is to protect the natural habitat of chimpanzees and to support research. The members also support protecting the environment as a whole. They work to educate people around the world with the hope that more people will take action, conserve the world's natural places, and protect the animals that live there.

Circle the letter of the best answer to the question below.

1. The Jane Goodall Institute

   a. is working to create safe habitats for chimps in the wild.

   b. has accomplished all of its goals and is no longer operating.

   c. believes that human beings have a responsibility to the environment.

   d. Both a and c

Write your answers on the lines below.

2. What scientific method of investigation did Goodall use during her field study?

   _____

3. Why was patience an important quality for Goodall to have as a scientist?

   _____

4. Why was Goodall's discovery that chimps could use tools so important?

   _____

   _____

5. What surprised scientists about Goodall's observation that two groups of chimps participated in a four-year war?

   _____

6. Why did Goodall name the chimps she studied? How was this different than the way most scientists worked?

   _____

   _____

7. What did Goodall notice about family groups of chimpanzees?

   _____

   _____

NAME _____

Review

Circle the letter of the best answer to each question below.

1. How are dangerous forms of radiation different from visible light?

    a. They have shorter wavelengths.

    b. They have longer wavelengths.

    c. They have wavelengths of only one color.

    d. Visible light doesn't contain any energy.

2. Who was the first human being to orbit Earth?

    a. Chuck Yeager

    b. Yuri Gagarin

    c. George Cayley

    d. Neil Armstrong

3. After the Chinese invented paper, they

    a. began using it in printing presses.

    b. sent examples of it to Italy with Marco Polo.

    c. tried to keep it a secret from the rest of the world.

    d. Both a and b

4. During their journey west, Lewis and Clark

    a. discovered plants and animals that had never been seen by human beings.

    b. made many scientific observations.

    c. experimented with growing new plants.

    d. All of the above

Write your answers on the lines below.

5. Give examples of two common beneficial uses of radiation.

    _____

6. Where do the names of most of the planets and constellations come from?

    _____

7. What is the focus of the SETI program?

    _____

8. Explain the Rare Earth hypothesis.

_____

9. Is Earth's gravity a powerful or weak force? Explain your answer.

_____

10. How did Henry Cavendish's shyness affect his work as a scientist?

_____

11. Why was Luther Burbank so well known for his work as a horticulturist?

_____

12. How did Burbank keep records of his work?

_____

13. Which do you think the Chinese invented first—gunpowder or rockets? Explain.

_____

14. Why was Jane Goodall's discovery that chimps use tools important?

_____

15. What was unique about Goodall's study of chimpanzees?

_____

16. Why was Lewis and Clark's expedition important to science?

_____

On the line, write the letter of the definition in column two that matches the word in column one.

17. _____ abacus   **a.** moving faster than the speed of sound

18. _____ sterilized   **b.** a frame with sliding beads used to make calculations

19. _____ field study   **c.** raised or developed

20. _____ cultivated   **d.** made a record by writing or drawing

21. _____ supersonic   **e.** a study of animals in their natural habitat

22. _____ patent   **f.** killed or removed living organisms

23. _____ documented   **g.** a license that gives the rights to an invention

Final Test

Write **true** or **false** next to each statement below.

1. _____ Most scientists agree that at one time, all of Earth's continents were joined together.

2. _____ Planet X turned out to be tiny Pluto.

3. _____ An object with potential energy has no inertia.

4. _____ The pendulum experiment showed that Earth's gravity pulls with the same force on all objects.

5. _____ The pH scale measures the amount of heat in a substance.

6. _____ Both plant cells and animal cells are surrounded by a cell wall.

7. _____ In most fossils, only the soft parts of plants and animals are preserved.

8. _____ Pluto has less than one percent of Earth's mass.

9. _____ The Big Bang theory explains how the universe will end with an explosion.

10. _____ Sonar produces ultrasound waves to map and locate objects underwater.

11. _____ Tunneling equipment changes depending on the type of material that needs to be tunneled through.

12. _____ If they are the same weight, a man and a woman will burn the same number of calories in a normal day.

13. _____ Paper was invented about 2,000 years ago in China.

Draw a line to match each scientist with his or her discovery or invention.

14. Nikola Tesla

15. Leonardo da Vinci

16. Jane Goodall

17. the Montgolfier Brothers

18. Luther Burbank

19. Henry Cavendish

20. Lewis and Clark

a. created hundreds of varieties of new plants

b. made the first successful public balloon flight

c. calculated a measurement of Earth's weight

d. added more than 200 plants and animals to the scientific record

e. developed an AC electrical power plant system

f. observed chimpanzees in the wild

g. designed a primitive helicopter

Underline the correct answer from the two choices you are given.

21. An experiment might be unsuccessful if it has too many (observations, variables).

22. Electron microscopes can only view objects that are good (conductors, insulators).

23. The exhaust coming out of a rocket gives the rocket (thrust, equilibrium).

24. Substances that have bound together chemically are (compounds, mixtures).

25. A substance with a pH of 10 is (basic, acidic).

26. Plants that have (fungi, spores) reproduce without seeds.

27. (Soldier, Worker) termites care for the eggs and tend to the needs of the colony.

28. (Erosion, Earthquakes) created the Grand Canyon.

29. The deepest ocean trenches are found where (subduction, volcanoes) occur(s).

30. Earth and the other planets share nearly the same plane of (tilt, orbit).

31. Calories are a measurement of the (kinetic, potential) energy in foods.

32. Harmful radiation can damage (DNA, membranes) inside cells.

33. The common names of most stars are (Greek, Arabic) in origin.

Write your answers on the lines below.

34. The isotope carbon-14 is used to date fossils like those found in the La Brea Tar Pits. What characteristic do isotopes have that makes this possible?

_____

35. Why can't electron microscopes view living organisms?

_____

36. Why did astronomers begin searching for a Planet X?

_____

_____

37. Briefly explain the theory of plate tectonics and its history.

_____

_____

_____

Final Test

38. How is the chain reaction in a nuclear reactor different from the one in an atomic explosion?

_____

39. Explain the difference between static electricity and an electrical current.

_____

40. What is natural selection?

_____

41. Where is DNA found, and what role does it play in cell function?

_____

_____

42. Why do social insects use pheromones?

_____

43. What role do baobab trees play in their ecosystem?

_____

44. Why are many animals in the Florida Everglades endangered?

_____

45. Human beings live in the troposphere. What makes it different than the other layers in Earth's atmosphere?

_____

46. What was human life like prior to the development of agriculture?

_____

47. What is nanotechnology?

_____

48. Why is it so important not to waste fresh water? Give at least two reasons.

_____

49. Why are colorful fruits and vegetables healthful?

_____

50. Name one risk and one benefit to living near a coast.

_____

51. What causes carpal tunnel syndrome?

_____

52. Explain Fermi's Paradox.

_____

53. What is the difference between a comet's common name and its scientific name?

_____

54. What kind of scientific investigations did Lewis and Clark do?

_____

Use the words in the box to complete the sentences below.

control	nitrogen submersibles	nozzles entropy	auroras calcium	photons eradicate

55. The _____ group in an experiment is often given a placebo or nothing at all.

56. Jonas Salk helped _____ polio in the United States.

57. The third law of thermodynamics states that everything moves toward _____.

58. _____ are tiny packets of energy in light and other forms of electromagnetic radiation.

59. _____ are attached to the open ends of rockets to make them more efficient.

60. Bacteria that "fix" _____ change it into a usable form for other living creatures.

61. _____ are created by the collision of solar wind with gases in Earth's atmosphere.

62. *Alvin* and other _____ help scientists study the deepest parts of the ocean.

63. Vitamin D makes _____ useful to your body.

Answer Key

Page 7

1. US
2. US
3. S
4. US
5. S
6. US

Possible answers:

7. Enrique should set the hot beaker somewhere other than beside the cold water.
8. Olivia should not smell the mixture unless her teacher told her it was okay.
9. Quinn should ask Danny to tell her about the movie later.
10. Darius should wash his hands and leave the lab area before touching his eyes.
11. so you don't accidentally consume something harmful
12. It could be a fire hazard, or it could touch the material you are working with.
13. Both groups wear special clothing or gear to protect their bodies.

Page 9

1. d
2. b
3. Possible answer: The radish seeds will grow best in the cup with soil and shredded bark.
4. the soil mixture
5. Possible answer: She will need to observe the seeds as they grow in order to draw a conclusion.
6. O
7. E
8. E
9. O

Page 11

Possible answers:

1. The boiling water will kill the yeast, so the balloon will not inflate.
2. The ice-cold water will not activate the yeast, so the balloon will not inflate.
3. The yeast will feed on the sugars in the grape juice, so they will produce carbon dioxide and the balloon will inflate.
4. The yeast will not eat the salt, so the balloon will not inflate.
5. You could add something acidic to the water, like lemon juice. You could add another sugary substance, like maple syrup to the water.
6. If you don't have a tight seal, the carbon dioxide could escape and the balloon would not inflate.
7. to keep the tiny pieces of yeast and sugar from spilling
8. Dry yeast is dormant.
9. carbon dioxide and alcohol

Page 13

1. b

2. c

3. d

4. The ice water made the glass surface cold. Air near the glass became cooled. The drop in temperature caused water molecules in the air to condense onto the glass surface.

5. Possible answer: At night, the temperatures outside dropped and cooled the window glass. Air inside the building cooled when it came near the glass, moisture in the air condensed onto the windows, and Julio's posters got wet.

Unifying Concepts and Processes

Possible answer: The temperature of the glass rose. Water from the air wasn't as cold as the glass, so it warmed the glass when it condensed there.

Page 15

1. d

2. c

3. Possible answer: Some animals came to drink water and became trapped in the sticky asphalt. Other animals tried to prey on the trapped animals and became trapped themselves.

4. It helps them form a complete picture of what life was like millions of years ago.

5. Possible answers: dental picks, cotton swabs, and toothbrushes

6. They compare the fossils they find with other fossils in the collection and with skeletons of modern animals.

7. Possible answer: If they keep everything organized, they will know what they have and where it is located when they want to study it at a later time.

Page 17

1. b

2. a

3. Possible answer: Scientists discovered seafloor spreading, which showed that parts of Earth's crust did move and what the cause of it was.

4. Possible answer: Animals that lived on Pangaea could roam across large parts of the continent. When Pangaea broke apart, the fossils of a type of animal living in one part of Pangaea ended up on more than one of the new continents.

5. Possible answer: Yes. He was a creative thinker. He kept believing in his ideas, even when others did not support him.

Page 19

1. c

2. a

3. Scientists had used math to calculate Uranus's orbit, but its actual orbit wasn't the same. They knew gravity from another planet had to be affecting Uranus's orbit.

4. Possible answer: Scientists can't control anything so far from Earth, so experiments are impossible.

5. Possible answer: Once spacecraft could fly to Neptune, a better measurement was taken of its mass and a Planet X was no longer necessary.

Unifying Concepts and Processes

Possible answer: Scientists used math to calculate what Uranus's and Neptune's orbits should be and then compared the calculations to the real orbits. Photographs that showed where objects in the sky appeared each night were used to see if any of them moved.

Page 21

1. d

2. b

3. Liquids and gases expand inside a vacuum, so the organism's shape would be destroyed.

4. Possible answer: They both magnify things that are too small to be seen otherwise.

5. Possible answer: Optical microscopes use light, but electron microscopes use electrons.

6. Possible answer: An optical microscope can view living organisms, but an electron microscope can only view dead organisms.

Page 23

1. epidemic

2. immunity

3. vaccine

4. eradicated

5. Possible answer: He needed to have one group that didn't receive the vaccine so he could compare the results with the group that did receive it.

6. Salk needed to see how many children would normally contract the disease.

7. a placebo

8. The viruses that Sabin used were live, weakened viruses.

Page 24

1. a

2. d

3. c

4. b

5. Chemicals could mix and a dangerous reaction could take place.

6. Observation allows scientists to ask questions about things around them, as well as understanding the results they get from experiments.

Page 25

7. sugar

8. Julio could see how the condensation that formed on the glass was the same thing that had happened on the windows when there was a change in temperature.

9. It helped them see the big picture of what life was like in an entire ecosystem millions of years ago.

10. The remains of certain fossils were found on more than one continent.

11. Possible answer: A placebo is a medicine that doesn't have any effect on a disease. It is given to subjects who think they are receiving actual medical treatment.

12. Molecules

13. vaccine

14. control

15. calculations

16. observation

17. organisms

18. vacuum

19. hypothesis

Page 27

1. b

2. c

3. Isotopes have more neutrons than a stable atom of the same element.

4. 146

5. Nuclear fission in an atomic bomb creates an uncontrolled chain reaction. The chain reaction in a nuclear reactor is controlled.

Unifying Concepts and Processes

Possible answer: Earth's age or the age of other objects in the solar system.

Page 29

1. c

2. b

3. d

4. the second law

5. Possible answer: The molecules in the sidewalk are excited because they have a lot of thermal energy. This thermal energy moves into the molecules of my feet, and I feel their increased thermal energy as heat.

6. Possible answer: My hand has more thermal energy than the ice cube, so energy flows out of my hand into the ice. The heat moving away from my hand makes my hand feel cold.

Page 31

1. a

2. c

3. c

4. light and heat emitted by the sun

5. Possible answer: Solar cells use photons in light to produce electricity. Mirrors and lenses create heat that can be used to make steam for turbines that produce electricity.

6. Solar power still costs a lot compared to the amount of energy it produces.

7. Possible answer: Yes. As fossil fuels become more expensive and solar cells get cheaper, using solar energy will be a good option.

Page 33

1. Possible answer: Newton's law says that an object in motion will continue moving at the same speed unless it is acted upon by an outside force. In a car accident, the impact would stop the car, but if you weren't buckled in, your body would fly through the air at a high speed.

2. Possible answer: If you kick a soccer ball, it will keep moving until friction with the ground and air molecules make it come to a stop.

3. Possible answer: A cup has rounded sides, so it rolls. Caleb needed to be able to mark the exact spot where the cup landed, so the boys needed to use an object that wouldn't roll.

4. When the skateboard hits the brick after gaining speed from rolling down the ramp, the skateboard will stop, but the box on top of it will continue moving.

Page 35

1. d

2. b

3. Possible answer: Static electricity builds up in your body, but when you get shocked, the electricity is no longer static—it's moving, which is an electrical current.

4. In the dry winter air, extra electrons aren't as likely to be absorbed into the air.

Page 37

1. Lift; thrust

2. air pressure

3. thermals

4. food; muscles

5. feathers

6. They are hollow.

7. When a bird soars, it doesn't have to flap its wings, an action that uses up energy.

8. Lift causes a bird to rise in the air, and thrust causes it to move forward.

9. Possible answer: The downstroke of a bird's wings pushes it forward. The upstroke is angled so the bird doesn't just hover in place.

Page 39

1. b

2. c

3. Potential energy, because the weight is not moving but it is suspended in the air.

4. Possible answer: As the weight swings, it has to push through the atoms and molecules in the air. This creates drag and friction that take away some of the pendulum's energy.

Page 41

1. a

2. b

3. They both contain the atoms of two or more elements.

4. A compound contains two or more elements that have combined chemically to form molecules. Mixtures contain two or more substances that have not combined chemically.

5. Table salt is a compound.

6. Possible answer: Alchemy was an ancient art that worked with metals. Chemistry is the modern, scientific study of chemicals and elements that grew out of alchemy.

Unifying Concepts and Processes

Possible answer: Chemical reactions need energy, and heat is energy on the move. Heating a substance is a simple way to give it the energy it needs to form or break chemical bonds.

Page 43

1. c

2. b

3. a

4. The baking soda is basic, or alkaline.

5. Most bacteria can't live in it, and bacteria are needed to make nutrients available to the plants.

6. acidic; less

7. Each unit represents a tenfold change, or a change by the power of 10.

Page 44

1. b

2. a

3. An isotope is an atom that has an unstable number of neutrons in its nucleus.

4. The chain reaction is uncontrolled in a nuclear explosion but carefully controlled in a nuclear reactor.

5. It gives them more energy, so they move around more quickly.

6. Because burning fossil fuels creates greenhouse gases, which are bad for the environment

Page 45

7. Possible answer: The photons in light can be used by a solar cell to create electricity.

8. Static electricity is when the electrical charge of matter has no place to go. An electrical current is electricity flowing.

9. Possible answer: The ball and your hand both have inertia as they move forward. When your hand stops, the ball's inertia continues to carry it forward.

10. Possible answer: Drag is a force that works against an object in motion. Friction can create drag.

11. They will swing at the same speed.

12. The different substances in the air can be easily separated because they aren't chemically bonded.

13. pH measures the concentration of hydrogen ions in a substance.

14. Atoms always try to return to a (<u>balanced</u>, unbalanced) state.

15. (<u>Thermodynamics</u>, Electromagnetism) is the study of how energy moves through the universe.

16. (Solar cells, <u>Photons</u>) are packets of energy in light.

17. Opposite charges (<u>attract</u>, repel) each other.

18. When the weight of a pendulum is in motion, it has (potential, <u>kinetic</u>) energy.

19. A propeller pulling an airplane through the air is an example of (lift, <u>thrust</u>).

20. A substance that is made up of molecules is a (mixture, <u>compound</u>) of at least two different elements chemically combined.

21. A substance that is neither an acid nor a base is (<u>neutral</u>, concentrated).

Page 47

1. a

2. c

3. b

4. red blood cells

5. Possible answer: They both contain organelles and nucleuses, and they divide to reproduce.

6. Possible answer: Plant cells are surrounded by cell walls, and they contain chlorophyll.

Page 49

1. d

2. d

3. There are species of plants and animals there that don't exist anywhere else in the world.

4. A new finch arrived on the island and began eating all the larger seeds. There was also a drought, which caused more competition for food.

5. Possible answer: Fewer of the light gray gypsy moths could survive without camouflage. The moths that were darker in color survived and reproduced. Over time, they took the place of the lighter gray moths.

Page 51

1. a

2. b

3. c

4. chromosomes

5. Possible answer: DNA contains the instructions that are used to create all the cells in an organism.

6. Possible answer: Each cell contains all the information needed to recreate an entire organism.

Page 53

1. c

2. A mushroom is a type of (spore, <u>fungus</u>).

3. Spores are how some organisms (<u>reproduce</u>, move).

4. Organisms like ferns and fungi have alternating (<u>generations</u>, cycles).

5. (Lichen, <u>Mold</u>) grows on food that has begun to decay.

6. It can be used to make cheese or medicine.

7. It doesn't look like the generation that comes before or after it.

8. spores

9. They are both methods for reproducing.

10. so that they can produce spores and the spores can spread

11. Possible answer: In most plants and animals, the young resemble the parent generation.

Page 55

1. true

2. false

3. true

4. false

5. false

6. true

7. to convert the nitrogen in the air and soil into a usable form

8. animal waste and decaying plant and animal material

9. Bacteria don't have a chance to convert the nitrates back into nitrogen gas, which can make the water dangerous for people and animals.

10. through rainwater and water used to irrigate crops

11. preying on herbivores

Unifying Concepts and Processes

Possible answer: The oxygen cycle; Both happen continuously, and both are necessary for life on Earth.

Page 57

1. c

2. d

3. They help the insects of the opposite sex find one another.

4. Possible answer: An insect of one species might use pheromones to lure and prey on an insect of another species.

5. Possible answer: They live in large groups, so communication is important in making community life work smoothly.

6. Possible answer: It's cleaner than using some pesticides.

7. Possible answer: They could send a warning about danger. They could tell others where food is located.

Page 59

1. true

2. false

3. false

4. true

5. false

6. true

Answer Key

7. A caste is a group that has a specific role within a society or community.

8. Answers will vary. Possible answer: They depend on each other for survival. A termite that lived alone might not be able to find food, defend itself, and reproduce.

9. reproduces   builds the nest   defends the colony

10. They eat wood and can destroy wooden structures.

11. Protozoa break the cellulose down into usable parts for the termites.

Unifying Concepts and Processes

Possible answer: Observing the termites' behavior over a period of time would give scientists the most information. They might also be able to use experimentation. For example, they could remove the queen to see how the colony is affected.

Page 61

1. a

2. b

3. They store water in the fibers for times of drought.

4. Possible answers: for food, for cloth, for medicine

5. Possible answers: They provide food, shelter, and water for animals in their ecosystem.

6. They help disperse the baobab's seeds.

7. Possible answers: The tree only blooms once a year, at night, so it has to attract bats and insects to it in order for pollination to take place.

8. to conserve energy when it is cold or very dry

Page 63

1. d

2. c

3. chemicals used in farming; mercury from burning fossil fuels

4. to create more farmland

5. Possible answer: Animals could go under the highway instead of across it, and the Everglades weren't cut in half by an impassible barrier.

6. Possible answer: People would probably continue to drain and pollute the Everglades as they built more homes and businesses. There would be less water available for drinking, and it wouldn't be clean.

Page 64

1. d

2. a

3. c

4. d

5. Possible answer: Plant cells have a cell wall. Animal cells do not.

6. Possible answer: Because all organisms are made up of cells

7. Their beaks allow them to perform different tasks, such as crushing seeds, carrying twigs, or pulling insects out of trees.

Page 65

8. Because every human being has thousands of genes.

9. To convert the nitrogen into a usable form

10. a message of danger   a message that tells where food can be found

11. Because every termite has a special role to play that allows the colony to function and survive.

12. Possible answers: The baobab has a thick trunk that can store lots of water. It is deciduous so it can conserve energy in times of drought.

13. Possible answer: food and medicine

14. The diversity of the plant and animal life and the fact that it contains so many environments in one place

15. true

16. true

17. false

18. false

19. false

20. false

21. true

22. true

Page 66

1. a

2. d

3. Possible answer: Don't eat or drink in the lab, and wear protective clothing when working with heat, chemicals, and glass.

4. Because the scientist can control the variables.

5. Some animals came to drink and became trapped in the asphalt. Other animals came to prey on them and became trapped as well.

6. They couldn't imagine something as large as a continent moving and didn't understand how it would move.

7. One group received the vaccine, one received a placebo, and one did not receive anything.

8. An ion has more or less electrons than protons, and an isotope has an unstable number of neutrons.

9. The car has more inertia. The heavier an object is, the more inertia it has.

Page 67

10. By the movement of electrons from one object to another when there is friction.

11. lift; thrust

12. When a pendulum is pulled back, gravity gives it potential energy, and when it is released, the potential energy is converted to kinetic energy.

13. lower; higher

14. Natural selection is the process by which organisms that are best suited to their environment pass along their beneficial traits to future generations.

15. They allow those organisms to reproduce.

16. Pheromones are chemicals that animals and insects release to communicate with others, usually of the same species.

17. Possible answer: Nitrogen is found in animal waste and decaying animal material. Animals take in nitrogen by eating plants or by eating other plant-eating animals.

18. Possible answers: They use it for food, shelter, and water.

19. c

20. e

21. a

22. g

23. b

24. f

25. d

Page 69

1. b

2. a

3. Possible answer: When scientists saw that seafloor spreading was creating the ridge, they realized Wegener's theory wasn't so far-fetched after all.

4. Possible answer: The continents and the ocean floor are both parts of the plates in Earth's crust.

5. Possible answer: The continents were all connected at one point, but because of seafloor spreading, they have been pushed apart.

Unifying Concepts and Processes

Possible answer: As two plates are pushed against each other, friction keeps them from moving smoothly and pressure builds up. This pressure is potential energy. When the plates finally move, the potential energy turns into kinetic energy, which is an earthquake.

Page 71

1. b

2. c

3. d

4. The movement of Earth's plates caused the Northern Rim to rise higher than the Southern Rim.

5. Possible answer: Yes. Erosion is still occurring at the Grand Canyon due to water freezing in the rocks and the flow of the Colorado River.

Unifying Concepts and Processes

Earth is at least, and probably much more than, two billion years old.

Page 73

1. d
2. d
3. false
4. true
5. false
6. false
7. true
8. It was the missing link between birds and reptiles.
9. Soft tissue of plants and animals was preserved.
10. They were discovered by quarry workers.
11. No, because the scavengers would have broken down more of the plant and animal remains.

Page 75

1. d
2. c
3. b
4. The weight of water creates pressure that prevents explosions.
5. Possible answer: Trenches are found where one tectonic plate is being driven underneath another plate.
6. Possible answer: Mauna Kea's base is located far below sea level on the ocean floor.

Page 77

1. a
2. b
3. c
4. between the mesosphere and thermosphere
5. Possible answer: Weather occurs in the troposphere, so it is much calmer and smoother to fly above it in the stratosphere.

Page 79

1. c
2. d
3. a
4. Solar wind is a stream of charged particles that the sun produces.
5. They can cause electrical disturbances and power outages.
6. Possible answer: Solar wind collides with Earth's atmosphere. When Earth's gases collide with solar particles, light is produced.
7. Possible answer: The conditions that create the auroras are never exactly the same. There are so many particles colliding at once, it would be impossible to have the exact same collisions take place again.

Page 81

1. a
2. b
3. a
4. b
5. Possible answer: Earth is tilted in relation to the sun, so as it orbits, Earth's top and bottom halves take turns being closest to the sun's warmth. When the top half is leaning toward the sun, it is summer in the Northern Hemisphere. When the top half is leaning away, it is summer in the Southern Hemisphere.

Page 83

1. c
2. a
3. c
4. Possible answer: Charon and Pluto orbit each other, which makes them a double planet.

Unifying Concepts and Processes

Possible answer: The nitrogen in Earth's atmosphere is a gas, while the nitrogen on Pluto's surface is frozen, making it a solid. The nitrogen on Pluto is frozen because Pluto is too far from the sun to receive much, if any, heat.

Page 85

1. c
2. d
3. Possible answer: Galaxies move too quickly based on the matter that can be seen, so dark matter has to make up the difference.
4. carbon and water
5. Possible answer: No. If there's other life out there, it's probably too far away to locate, and if that life doesn't know how to communicate, it won't contact us either.

Page 86

1. d
2. b
3. c
4. b
5. seafloor spreading
6. volcanoes and earthquakes

Page 87

7. An island is created.
8. It was undersea at one time.
9. They show soft tissues that aren't usually recorded in other fossils.
10. It stops most of the sun's ultraviolet radiation from reaching the surface.

11. nitrogen

12. The aurora borealis occurs in the Northern Hemisphere. The aurora australis occurs in the Southern Hemisphere.

13. The tilt creates Earth's seasons.

14. Charon is very large compared to Pluto, and the two objects orbit each other.

15. Possible answer: The universe began as a single, dense particle that exploded.

16. mantle

17. sediments

18. subduction

19. precession

20. Cosmology

Page 89

1. b

2. d

3. Possible answer: No. Early human beings cleared the land to make hunting easier and to make more room for edible wild plants to grow.

4. They produce seeds.

5. Possible answer: Domesticated animals meant that human beings didn't have to hunt, and they had animals that could be used for labor.

Page 91

1. c

2. b

3. V-2 rockets traveled faster than sound.

4. Possible answer: The force of exhaust leaving the rocket creates an equal and opposite force that pushes the rocket forward.

Unifying Concepts and Processes

1. Possible answer: Blocking the end of a hose makes the water shoot out with more power, and it travels farther. The nozzle on the end of a rocket forces the exhaust through a narrower space, so it shoots out with greater force and propels the rocket with more force.

2. Possible answer: No. A rocket could use air that's under pressure, like a balloon that shoots around the room if it hasn't been tied at the end.

Page 93

1. b

2. a

3. The electrons in a direct current flow in one direction. The electrons in an alternating current move back and forth very quickly.

4. The AC power from the outlet has to be changed into DC power.

5. 0.5 amps

Answer Key

6. 600 watts

7. 240 volts

Page 95

1. c

2. d

3. c

4. the time it takes an ultrasound wave to travel from the probe and return as an echo

5. Possible answer: Both sonar and ultrasound use sound waves to "see" things, but sonar sound waves are big enough to be heard by human beings, while ultrasound waves are too small.

6. Possible answer: Both radar and ultrasound imaging use waves to create images, but radar uses radio waves, and ultrasound uses sound waves.

7. There is much less risk using ultrasound than radioactive X-rays.

Page 97

1. b

2. Answers will vary.

3. Possible answer: It is stronger because it contains folded cardboard between the layers. This allows it to spread weight out over a greater surface.

4. Possible answer: Yes, the bridges would be weaker if the boxes were spaced farther apart.

5. The students' accordion-style bridge used a similar concept. The truss bridge gets some of its strength from the triangle shape of the supports.

Page 99

1. c

2. a

3. true

4. false

5. false

6. true

7. to carry clean water into cities and transport sewage away

8. Possible answer: It was probably hard to move and could collapse easily. The workers froze it to make it easier to move.

9. Possible answer: Moles are safer and quieter and leave behind a smoother tunnel.

Page 101

1. c

2. b

3. They wanted to see whether it was possible to breathe at a high altitude.

4. Possible answer: The pilot changes altitude and catches a wind current that is moving in the direction he or she wants to travel.

5. Possible answer: You can't steer a hot air balloon or make it move very quickly.

6. Possible answer: The pilot can turn the propane off and on. The amount of heat determines whether the balloon will rise or fall.

Unifying Concepts and Processes

Possible answer: Something that floats must be lighter, or less dense, than the substance that surrounds it, whether it is air or water.

Page 103

1. submersible

2. porthole

3. manipulators

4. pressure

5. Steel weights drag *Alvin* down to the ocean floor. To return to the surface, the pilot releases the weights.

6. They both allow human beings to travel to places they could never go without the use of technology.

7. Possible answer: It's important to make sure that all the parts are working because the passengers' lives could be in danger if something didn't work properly deep underwater.

8. The manipulators can gather samples for the scientists, who can't leave the sub because the pressure deep underwater is too intense.

Unifying Concepts and Processes

Possible answer: Yes, because the conditions deep underwater are extreme, just as they are on other planets.

Page 105

1. c

2. a

3. d

4. Possible answer: Larger materials are carved or etched down to create materials in the nanoscale.

5. Possible answer: Nanoscale materials are built by combining individual atoms.

6. Possible answer: Yes. If nanoscale machines can be built, the number of things they might be able to do could completely change the world.

Page 106

1. c

2. d

3. b

4. Possible answer: Human beings were able to stay in one place, which allowed them to build things like houses and roads.

5. Possible answer: Before agriculture, human beings spent nearly all of their time hunting and gathering food. Agriculture allowed other skills to be developed.

6. Possible answer: Exhaust shooting out of the end of a rocket propels the rocket in the opposite direction because every force creates an equal and opposite force.

7. Possible answer: He thought AC was too powerful and dangerous to use.

Answer Key

8. Ultrasound waves have a frequency too high to hear.

9. Possible answer: The probe emits ultrasound waves, and then it receives ultrasounds that return as echoes. The machine measures how long this takes and creates images based on the measurements.

10. They altered the paper's shape.

11. Possible answers: to transport water and to hold electrical lines

12. Possible answer: Moles are much quieter, safer, and more precise.

13. The air inside the balloon is less dense, and therefore lighter, than the surrounding air.

14. Sunlight doesn't reach that far below the ocean's surface.

15. Possible answer: to make the chemicals in sunscreen

16. Before agriculture, human beings (foraged, traded) for the food they needed to survive.

17. The (fuel, exhaust) shooting out of a rocket propels it forward.

18. Electrical appliances that plug into outlets use (AC, DC) electricity.

19. An electrical current's speed is measured in (watts, amps).

20. (Radar, sonar) uses radio waves to locate objects and create images of them.

21. Modern hot air balloons use (methane, propane) fuel as the source of their heat.

22. The materials used to build a bridge are considered to be the (live, dead) load.

23. A nanometer is one (millionth, billionth) of a meter.

Page 109

1. a

2. the amount of potential energy a food contains

3. If your body doesn't use all the energy a food provides, the calories are converted to fat and stored.

4. Because someone who is very active will burn a lot more calories than someone who isn't active at all.

5. 2, 4, 1, 3

Page 111

1. d

2. Water-soluble vitamins don't get stored in the body for long, so they need to be replenished every day. Fat-soluble vitamins are stored in the body for days or months.

3. Sailors got scurvy because they didn't eat fresh produce for long periods of time. Possible answer: People who live in extreme poverty or who don't have access to fresh produce might be at risk today.

4. Possible answers: fish, milk, spinach, eggs

5. Possible answers: Because different foods contain different vitamins and you need to eat a wide variety of foods to get all the vitamins your body needs

6. The recommended daily allowance tells you how much of each vitamin your body needs each day.

Page 113

1. false

2. true

3. false

4. false

5. true

6. Possible answer: It would be almost impossible to build an earthquake-proof building, but many buildings are able to resist earthquakes.

7. Possible answer: It can be expensive. Some changes might be hard to make to older, existing buildings.

8. Possible answer: They can try to figure out why the buildings were damaged and how to prevent that sort of damage in the future.

9. They can absorb some of the motion or movement from an earthquake.

10. Possible answer: They probably choose locations where large numbers of people could be in danger if a structure collapsed.

11. Possible answer: Structures that are flexible won't snap or break as easily.

Page 115

1. b

2. Possible answer: The time and effort it takes to find or create clean water takes away from time that could be spent earning a living or getting an education.

3. Possible answer: As water levels decrease because of the drought, the concentration of pollutants in the water increases, making the water even more unhealthy.

4. Possible answer: Water that soaks into the ground mixes with the buried garbage in a landfill. As the water moves deeper underground, it carries chemicals from the garbage down into the aquifer.

5. Possible answer: Yes. The government should make sure that one person or business doesn't use up all of a limited resource, or there won't be any of it left for the rest of the population.

Page 117

1. Possible answers: watering plants, cleaning, experiments

2. Possible answer: The water coming out of a hot water faucet has been heated, which means fossil fuels or another energy source is being wasted, not just water.

3. 21,600

4. Possible answer: I let the water run while I brush my teeth, so I should shut it off. When I let the water run to get it hot, I should put a cup or bowl in the sink to catch the unused water. It can be used for watering plants.

Unifying Concepts and Processes

Possible answer: The sewage has to be treated before it is dumped back into a river or other waterway, and this process is not free.

Page 119

1. d

2. They arrived in America by boat, and fish was a plentiful source of food.

3. Possible answer: Beach property is in high demand, and wildlife is being pushed out.

4. Possible answers: You can enjoy the wildlife, you can fish, you can surf or swim.

5. Global warming is causing glaciers and ice caps to melt. The extra water causes sea levels to rise.

6. Because the human population in those areas is increasing.

Unifying Concepts and Processes

Possible answer: There is a limited amount of oil. When the amount of oil decreases, gas prices go up. People will need to find alternatives to using oil.

Page 121

1. There are more Internet users in (China, <u>the United States</u>) than any other country.

2. Today, the rates of Internet use around the world are (<u>growing</u>, remaining steady).

3. The Internet makes information more available to (wealthy people, <u>nearly everyone</u>).

4. If you visit (a WiFi café, <u>an Internet café</u>) you do not need to bring a computer with you.

5. Possible answer: They both made a lot of information available to a large group of people.

6. Possible answer: The Internet allows scientists to quickly share information. It also allows them to do research and work with one another over long distances.

7. Because scientists build on each other's knowledge.

8. Possible answer: Information allows people to educate themselves and have more opportunities in life. The same information is available to everyone online, so they all have an equal chance to learn.

9. Possible answer: People wouldn't receive and use the information as quickly, and it wouldn't be so widespread.

Page 123

1. c

2. pain, numbness, and weakness in the arm and wrist

3. They are all people who do repeated motion with their hands and arms.

4. Possible answer: The pressure on his wrist and arm could lead to carpal tunnel syndrome if he regularly works at that computer.

5. It can give your body a break and help you avoid computer-related injuries.

6. Their eyes try to focus on the pixels on a computer screen, and they don't blink as often as they should.

7. Possible answer: People who spend a lot of time at the computer aren't being very active, so they aren't burning many calories. They could try to take frequent breaks to get up and move around, or they could make an effort to be very active when they are not on the computer.

Page 125

1. Possible answer: Growing crops meant that some people could spend their time doing things other than foraging for food. New skills and occupations grew from this change.

2. Possible answers: automobiles, rubber, ovens

3. Possible answers: auto mechanic, car part manufacturer

4. Possible answers: worker in a water treatment plant

5. Possible answer: Fewer people needed to be employed because one person on a tractor could do the work of many people.

6. Answers will vary.

Page 126

1. b

2. c

3. c

4. false

5. true

6. false

7. true

8. true

9. false

10. true

Page 127

11. calories in foods that have little or no nutritional value

12. You will be sure to get all the vitamins, minerals, and other nutrition your body needs.

13. Because your body doesn't store water-soluble vitamins.

14. Possible answer: They examine the damage on similar buildings that have experienced an earthquake.

15. Possible answer: They have built buildings on springs or rollers.

16. Ninety-seven percent of water is saltwater, which is not drinkable. Fresh water that is polluted also limits the amount of drinkable water.

17. The constant drip from a leaking faucet can quickly add up to a lot of wasted water.

18. It destroys habitat and causes pollution.

19. Both the printing press and the Internet increased the speed and amount of information that scientists could access and learn from.

20. You should sit up straight with your hips and head in a straight line. Your elbows should form a right angle, and you shouldn't lean your wrist on the mouse pad.

21. Possible answer: freezer; someone who works in an ice-cream parlor

Page 129

1. c

2. d

3. d

4. Possible answer: Radiation can be used to kill cancer cells, but it can also damage good cells.

Unifying Concepts and Processes

Possible answer: Radiation damages the DNA inside cells' nucleuses. DNA contains genetic material and cell growth, so damaged DNA can cause defects.

Page 131

1. true

2. false

3. true

4. false

5. true

6. Possible answers: An object in the sky; the moon and Venus.

7. They used the names of people from their myths.

8. the IAU

9. Possible answer: Their common names come from the people, groups, or instruments that discovered them. A comet's scientific name is the year of discovery and a letter telling the order of its discovery that year.

10. Possible answer: They were named after people, animals, or objects they resembled.

Page 133

1. b

2. search for extra-terrestrial intelligence

3. Possible answer: The universe is massive and old, so it would seem to make sense that other intelligent life exists other than human beings. However, there has never been any sign of it.

4. Possible answer: Intelligent life evolved on Earth only because of a series of highly unlikely events, so intelligent life is not at all common in the universe.

5. Possible answer: If a pattern is unnatural, then it was created on purpose, which would indicate that the creator is intelligent. Whether we understand the signal or not doesn't matter.

6. Possible answer: It's not a wasted effort. The evidence of a signal might show up in 50, 60, or 70 years, and stopping now would mean we would never hear it.

Page 135

1. place a check mark beside: Human beings orbited Earth.

2. place a check mark beside: The first jumbo jet flight took place.

3. place a check mark beside: Kites were invented.

4. place a check mark beside: Planes were used in wartime.

5. They studied the flight of birds.

6. Planes were used in spying and in warfare.

7. Possible answer: The Wright Brothers' plane was actually a glider with an engine. George Cayley had spent many years perfecting the glider.

8. Possible answer: I think that there will be progress in space flight. Maybe it will be faster or safer, or more people will have the opportunity to travel in space.

Unifying Concepts and Processes

Possible answer: A space shuttle is so complex that a large number of people probably had to work together to create it.

Page 137

1. c

2. d

3. Possible answer: Cavendish didn't like to be around people, which meant that he spent more time working in his lab and doing lots of research.

4. Possible answer: He didn't share his knowledge or research, so other scientists spent years looking for answers Cavendish had already discovered.

Page 139

1. patent

2. horticulturist

3. bred

4. cultivate

5. when it has been bred to have certain characteristics

6. They didn't think his methods of data collection were very scientific.

7. Possible answer: He used photos as a way to keep track of his plants and compare them. Photography helped Burbank with his scientific investigations.

8. Possible answers: potatoes, daisies, roses, cacti

9. Possible answers: He wanted them to be full of flavor and last a long time.

Page 141

1. c

2. c

3. Possible answer: They already had reliable methods of navigating by using the sun and the stars.

4. Possible answer: They both looked for ways to turn ordinary metals into gold.

5. Possible answer: Scientific knowledge from China made its way to Europe, where the scientists built upon what they learned from the Chinese.

Unifying Concepts and Processes

Possible answer: Solar objects, like stars and planets, appear as dots of light. Knowing the exact time these objects appear in the sky helps astronomers keep track of what they are seeing.

Page 143

1. b

2. Possible answer: A carefully written record of what they saw would be more believable and reliable.

3. observation and collecting evidence

4. Possible answer: Zoologists can't study or learn about animals that haven't been discovered yet.

5. Possible answer: Knowledge of the Western landscape allowed others to make detailed maps of the area, which could be used by future travelers.

6. Possible answer: People began hunting and killing the animals in large numbers, so the wildlife evolved to have a fear of human beings.

Unifying Concepts and Processes

Possible answer: These scientists could observe new plants and animals and add to the body of scientific knowledge about the world.

Page 145

1. d

2. observation

3. Possible answer: She had to wait a long time before the chimps were comfortable so that they would come near enough to be observed.

4. Possible answer: Until then, scientists thought only human beings used tools. The fact that chimpanzees did as well meant that a new definition of *human being* needed to be found.

5. Possible answer: Scientists didn't think any animal but human beings engaged in warfare.

6. Goodall named the chimps because she thought they had individual personalities and behaviors. Most scientists give their subjects numbers instead of names.

7. They had many behaviors that were similar to human family interactions.

Page 146

1. a

2. b

3. c

4. b

5. Possible answers: X-rays and cancer treatment

6. Greek and Roman mythology

7. searching for extra-terrestrial intelligence

Page 147

8. Intelligent life is extremely rare and arose on Earth only because of a series of unlikely events.

9. Possible answer: It's a weak force. Any time an object is picked up or moved, you are overcoming the force of an entire planet pulling against the object.

10. Possible answer: Cavendish had a lot of time to spend on research, but he didn't share his results like a scientist should always do.

11. Because he created more than 800 varieties of plants

12. He made notes, took photos of his plants and fruits, and made impressions of certain fruits on notecards.

13. Possible answer: Gunpowder had to have been invented first because it was used as a fuel in the rockets.

14. Possible answer: Scientists had thought that only human beings used tools before Goodall's discovery was made.

15. Possible answer: She gave her scientific subjects names rather than simply numbering them.

16. Possible answer: They added many species of plants and animals to the scientific record.

17. b

18. f

19. e

20. c

21. a

22. g

23. d

Page 148

1. true

2. false

3. true

4. true

5. false

6. false

7. false

8. true

9. false

10. false

11. true

12. false

13. true

14. draw a line to e

15. draw a line to g

16. draw a line to f

17. draw a line to b

18. draw a line to a

19. draw a line to c

20. draw a line to d

Page 149

21. An experiment might be unsuccessful if it has too many (observations, <u>variables</u>).

22. Electron microscopes can only view objects that are good (<u>conductors</u>, insulators).

23. The exhaust coming out of a rocket gives the rocket (<u>thrust</u>, equilibrium).

24. Substances that have bound together chemically are (<u>compounds</u>, mixtures).

25. A substance with a pH of 10 is (<u>basic</u>, acidic).

26. Plants that have (fungi, <u>spores</u>) reproduce without seeds.

27. (Soldier, <u>Worker</u>) termites care for the eggs and tend to the needs of the colony.

28. (<u>Erosion</u>, Earthquakes) created the Grand Canyon.

29. The deepest ocean trenches are found where (<u>subduction</u>, volcanoes) occur(s).

30. Earth and the other planets share nearly the same plane of (tilt, <u>orbit</u>).

31. Calories are a measurement of the (kinetic, <u>potential</u>) energy in foods.

32. Harmful radiation can damage (<u>DNA</u>, membranes) inside cells.

33. The common names of most stars are (Greek, <u>Arabic</u>) in origin.

34. They decay at a steady rate and turn into different substances.

35. The object to be viewed with an electron microscope has to be put into a vacuum.

36. The orbits of Uranus and Neptune didn't match the astronomers' calculations.

37. Possible answer: Wegener looked at the continents' shapes and the fossil record and knew that all of Earth's land was once joined together. Today, scientists know that the lithosphere is broken up into tectonic plates and seafloor spreading pushes the plates around.

Page 150

38. In a nuclear reactor, the chain reaction is controlled. In an atomic explosion, it is not.

39. The extra electrons in a static charge don't go anywhere. In an electrical current, they move from atom to atom.

40. Natural selection is the process by which organisms pass along their most beneficial traits to future generations.

41. DNA is located in the nucleus of a cell. DNA contains the genetic information that controls a cell's reproduction and growth.

42. Possible answers: to attract mates and to warn or guide other insects

43. Possible answer: They provide water and shelter.

44. Because human beings have damaged or destroyed much of their habitat.

45. Weather occurs in the troposphere because it contains most of the atmosphere's gases and water vapor.

46. Human beings spent most of their time hunting or gathering food.

47. Building materials at the nanoscale, which is based on the nanometer, or one-billionth of a meter

48. Possible answer: Only one percent of Earth's water is thawed fresh water, so it is a limited resource. Other limited resources are used to make water clean enough to drink.

Page 151

49. They contain lots of vitamins that the human body needs to function.

50. Possible answers: Hurricanes are a risk. Eating fresh fish is a benefit.

51. doing a repeated motion with your hands over a long period of time

52. The universe is huge and old, so it makes sense that intelligent life other than human beings exists, but there has never been any sign of it.

53. A comet's common name is usually the name of the scientist who discovered it. Its scientific name is a series of numbers that tell when it was discovered.

54. They collected samples and recorded information about the plants and animals they observed.

55. control

56. eradicate

57. entropy

58. Photons

59. Nozzles

60. nitrogen

61. Auroras

62. submersibles

63. calcium